The Landscape of Ideas

The Landscape of Ideas

PATRICK NUTTGENS

FABER AND FABER LIMITED
3 Queen Square, London

First published in 1972
by Faber and Faber Limited
3 Queen Square, London WC1
Printed in Great Britain
by W & J Mackay Limited, Chatham
All rights reserved

ISBN 0 571 09186 5

Acknowledgments

This book formed the Annual Lectures delivered in 1967–68 to the *Institute for the Study of Worship and Religious Architecture* in the University of Birmingham under the title: 'The Landscape of Ideas: Sacred and Secular'.

Chapters 2 and 4 were based on material prepared for lectures at the Royal Institute of British Architects under the title 'The Man Made Environment' in 1963.

Chapter 3 was first delivered as a lecture to the Art Workers Guild under the title 'Architecture and the Metaphysics of Light' in 1965.

★

Acknowledgments are due to the author and Yale University Press for permission to quote from *The Earth, the Temple and the Gods* by Vincent Scully.

★

Acknowledgments are made to the following photographers: Aerofilms Ltd. for illustration nos. 1, 2a and b, 4, 14a and b, 19, 30, 31, 43 and 45; the Conway Library at the Courtauld Institute for 12; Martin Butlin for 18; F. Mella for 8; C. J. Balmforth for 9; A. F. Kersting for 10, 11, 20, 22, 23 and 29; the British Travel Association for 3, 24 and 33; The Trustees of the British Museum for 34; Keith Gibson for 16, 26a, 27, 35, 36, 37, 38, 39, 40, 41 and 42; the Mansell Collection for 7 and 17; the French Government Tourist Office for 21; the German State Archaeological Institute for figure 1.

Contents

Illustrations

Introduction

The theme of this book is the effect on the physical environment of certain ideas at different periods of history. The interpretation of history in terms of the history of ideas is a relatively modern study; its growth may reflect a need to synthesise increasingly diverse and specialised areas of investigation. In any case, it is especially relevant to studies of the physical environment: the landscape, its buildings, its towns and villages, and the social, economic and aesthetic factors that influence its form.

'It was His Majesty, my Commander-in-Chief, who set the Thames on fire. It was he who invented gunpowder and stole fire from the gods. He nearly blew the whole place up. But he caught the pieces and tied them together again with string. He was the one who fitted up the first forges on earth. He discovered the way to make steel. He used to work eighteen hours a day and he made *us* work even harder. He was our chief engineer. As an engineer he made the first balloon, and then the Zeppelin and finally, with his own hands, he built the first aeroplane. At the start it wasn't a success. The first test pilots, Icarus and the rest, all fell into the sea. Till eventually he piloted the plane himself . . . Long before that, when he was only a little prince, he'd invented the wheelbarrow. . . . Then rails and automobiles. He drew up the plans for the Eiffel Tower, not to mention his designs for the sickle and the plough, the harvesters and the tractors . . .

'He extinguished volcanoes and caused new ones to erupt. He built Rome, New York, Moscow and Geneva. He *founded* Paris. He created revolutions, counter-revolutions, religion, reform, and counter-reform.

'He wrote tragedies and comedies, under the name of Shakespeare. . . . It was a secret.

'He invented the telephone and the telegraph, and fixed them up himself. He did everything with his own hands . . .

'Not so long ago he managed to split the atom.

Majesty, Commander-in-Chief, Master, Managing Director . . .'[1]

These juxtaposed passages are from Ionesco's play, *Exit the King*. The King is dying; he has only a few moments left before he will fade from the scene. The catalogue of his achievements comes from his guard, and at first it seems improbable, to say the least. It is none the less relevant, not only to the king, but to all of us; for Beranger the King is Everyman, as Everyman is king of his private world. And the dying king is the dying of any human mind, the stripping, piece by piece, of its consciousness until there is nothing left but nothing.

The achievements in the catalogue are his—or ours—because of his—and our—consciousness of them. We live each in a little world, and it is a world of our own making, which depends upon us individually for its continuance. The things which we know about are, in a sense, invented by us because they are part of our knowledge and our awareness. We live, in a sense, in our own personal environments; and in that sense, the environment of every man is his own creation.

That is what I mean by the 'Landscape of Ideas'. The landscape in its widest sense, the *environment*, is literally our surroundings. It is the backcloth against which we can measure the importance of our activities and the scale of our personalities. It is everything which we are not. It is the physical setting of our lives, the moral and intellectual climate in which we work out our destinies, the emotional wilderness or tamed landscape of feeling within which we develop the particularity of our experiences. Yet it is of our making; and we are part of a process, shared with our ancestors and our descendants, which modifies our surroundings at every moment in time.

This naturally makes the landscape peculiarly difficult to describe and almost impossible to define. At a simpler period of history, one might have studied it as something static, with oneself as a static observer. Like Renaissance perspective, it could take its shape as something fixed in time and space, subject to reasonable laws. Renaissance perspective assumed, indeed, that the observer was stationary in one place. But in a world that has been changed by the theories of Einstein

[1] E. Ionesco, *Exit the King*, in Collected Works, Vol. 5, London, 1963.

and the vision of Picasso, we know that perspective obeys no such laws, that both the objects observed and the person observing them are in constant but irregular movement, in a changing relation with each other.

This may partly explain a change that has occurred in recent historical works on architecture and urban form. Until recently, architectural history was mainly studied and taught as the history of styles; guide books are still frequently spotters' guides to periods and their characteristics. But research in greater depth has revealed more profound reasons for the widespread emergence or acceptance of specific building types and their forms; in such works as, for example, Vincent Scully's *The Earth the Temple and the Gods*, Otto von Simson's *The Gothic Cathedral*, and (from a different professional background) Harvey Cox's *The Secular City*.

In these and other works the analysis reveals the existence of an intellectual background, or a conceptual framework, which fundamentally affected the way in which the physical environment took shape. But, by implication, such frameworks also emphasise the way in which the writer or observer 'makes'— or projects—history from his own preconceptions. Within the last few generations the techniques of discovery and the number of people making discoveries of the past have increased significantly. But specialisms are often rigid. Archaeologists have been described as studying a special little world in which the spade cannot lie. But even if the spade cannot lie, as a historian remarked, that may be only because it cannot speak either.

As our knowledge increases, it is all the more difficult to take a total view of the landscape; yet the old urge to do so persists.

In the latter part of the nineteenth century, when the land had been transformed by the growth of monster industrial cities, gulping down hills and valleys, swallowing rivers and belching smoke from a gargantuan digestion of energising material, it became for a while fashionable to hire a balloon and drift up into the air for a look at things. The 'balloon view' took the observer away from an obsession with details. In his book on Victorian cities, Asa Briggs quotes two such observers writing in 1862. 'It was a wonderful sight,' they said, 'to behold that vast bricken mass of churches and hospitals, banks and prisons, palaces and workhouses, docks and refuges for the destitute, parks and squares, and courts and alleys, which make up London—all blent into one immense black spot—to look down upon the whole as the birds of the air look down upon it, and see it dwindled into a mere rubbish heap—to contemplate from afar that strange conglomeration of vice and avarice and low cunning, of noble aspirations and human heroism, and to grasp it in the eye, in all its incongruous integrity, at a single glance—to take, as it were, an angel's view of that huge town where, perhaps, there is more virtue and more iniquity, more wealth and more want, brought together into one dense focus than in any other points of the earth.'[1]

It was a similar, but more thoughtful, enthusiasm that led Sir Patrick Geddes in 1910 to establish in Edinburgh the Outlook Tower and the Camera Obscura. Tourists today can visit the rooms that once housed exhibits illustrating the state of the World, Europe, Britain and Edinburgh, floor by floor in ascending order, and watch in the huge saucer of the Camera Obscura activities taking place at that moment in the streets and wynds and closes of that stern city. But to Geddes it was far more than the novelty advertised today as 'Nature's TV'. Geddes was a pioneer of modern sociology, and the pioneer of modern town and regional planning. Omnivorous for facts, volubly enthusiastic for their arrangement, he pleaded above all for a 'synoptic' view of our cities and towns. Such a view does not come easily. A synoptic view requires a synoptic kind of mind, and most people are probably better at analysis than at synopsis. Yet it forms an essential ingredient in any systematic process of town and country planning—an activity in whose genesis Geddes was a seminal figure.

At a time when building and rebuilding are proceeding on an unprecedented scale, and when a whole area can be reorganised and replanned in all its aspects, it seems useful to examine the ideas or intentions of the people responsible for building at other times in history. Such ideas inevitably vary in kind and scope under different conditions; they may be clear, deliberate and formulated; they may be vague but nevertheless pervasive; they may have the character of *idées reçus*. It is clear to me that a number of them have effectively shaped the landscape and the pattern of people's lives. An understanding of them must be helpful in assessing what are the ideas determining the changing character of regions, towns and buildings today.

I have therefore selected certain periods for examination—the Functional Environment, the Greek, Mediaeval and Renaissance settings, and, in the last two chapters, the transformation of the world in the nineteenth and twentieth

[1] Asa Briggs, *Victorian Cities*, London 1963, p. 53.

centuries. Both countryside and towns are discussed; but if there is a bias towards town rather than country it is easily explained. For 'the civic arts', as Lethaby remarked, 'are the arts of civilization, and the arts of civilization are civilization itself'.[1]

[1] W. R. Lethaby, *Form in Civilization*, London 1900, p. 100.

1 The Functional Environment

In looking at the Functional Environment, it is best to start with the country. 'God made the country and man made the town', Cowper wrote; and it may be suitably deferential to start with God and come round to man later—a development that seems to be characteristic of civilizations. The very beginnings of the landscape are dictated by the way in which Man has reacted to the difficulties and challenges of Nature. The demand is for survival and improvement, and in an unsophisticated world the shapes and forms of man-made places are explained almost wholly by his reaction to his condition. The Functional Environment is the simplest, most primitive and most lasting kind; it is the environment shaped by functional needs and limitations imposing a rigorous organisation upon Man.

How does this happen?

'Human Life', wrote Lewis Mumford, 'swings between two poles: movement and settlement.'[1] The process whereby people in specific regions become settled, in contrast to their nomadic contemporaries, need not be elaborated; it is related to developments in agriculture and political circumstances, to the agricultural revolutions of prehistory (for instance) that translated some places of hunting into places of tillage.

As soon as settlement becomes necessary, the first lines of an organised environment have been laid down. They are lines, sometimes literal ones, that can be traced along the landscape—lines of terraces, limits of cultivation, or traces of buildings. In Great Britain it is not necessary to explore prehistory; the framework of our surroundings dates effectively from the work of the Anglo-

[1] Lewis Mumford, *The City in History*, London 1961, p. 5.

Saxon village settlers in the middle of the fifth century.

From that moment the landscape, taken for granted and even sometimes assumed to be 'natural', can be seen as a series of overlays by successive waves of settlement, elaborating and diversifying a basic village pattern. Whatever happened in subsequent major land changes, with the Danish invasion, the Norman colonisation, the late mediaeval rebuilding, the eighteenth-century agricultural revolution, even with the urban explosion of the nineteenth and twentieth centuries, the village network was fundamental.

The basic distinction between types of settlement is that between *dispersed* and *nucleated*. The distinction is not always clear because there are often marginal cases (and every year there are more) when it is difficult to decide whether a place is somewhat nucleated or partially dispersed. Nevertheless it is useful and provides a framework for this discussion; for it emphasises the influence of specific work and specific place on the developing character of the built forms.

The *dispersed* settlement is a collection of relatively isolated dwellings, separated in regular or varying distances by the fields with which the dwellings are concerned, either singly or jointly. In such a settlement there is no dominant and no particular form other than that of the individual dwellings themselves. Almost everything in it is dictated by natural demands; the dwellings may lie on a certain contour above flood level, but any consistent form of grouping can only be read into it, and is little more than a statistical summary. It represents Nature more or less dominant.

The *nucleated* settlement is more contrived, has a more complex history and is the subject of the rest of this chapter. It has a focus, many different forms, and can be related to its functional origins. Its character depends significantly on its specific geographical setting and on its economic function. It is therefore important to ask what kind of settlement it is.

Size does not provide an adequate definition. There are villages of two hundred people in parts of Western Europe, and villages of 20,000–30,000 inhabitants in the Hungarian steppes; there are hamlets of ten inhabitants in Flanders, and 500 inhabitants in Italy.

Categorisation by function is more satisfactory; for the influence of the agrarian system upon types of settlement is fundamental. To simplify a complex process, it may be said that communal open-field agricultural methods required the establishment of a nucleated village system, whereas individual cultivation of plots of land automatically led to the isolated farmstead—in other words the system of land tenure is what determines the physical layout, and thus the character, of the man-made environment. The village system was the logical outcome of communal ownership of land. From that village system there grew, under Celtic, Germanic and later Slavonic ethnic influences, the 'runddorf' or round village and the 'strassendorf' or street village. Both types can be seen in Britain.[1]

But while the agrarian system and land tenure will account for the basic type of settlement, it is not enough to explain the particular shape and special character. Equally important are such factors as water supply, relief, soils, insolation, defence, administration and special legislation which help to explain the specific patterns of settlements—at certain contours, on certain slopes, with a certain orientation, and within a certain network of communications. Ultimately, however, it is work that counts; it is possible to connect settlement types with different kinds of work—to distinguish, for example, villages that grew out of the clearing of forests from those developing in other ways. In England place-names give some evidence. Villages whose names end in '-den', '-falt', '-hold', '-werst' and -'ward' are said to indicate the process of clearing forests which was fairly continuous up to the middle of the fourteenth century.

But from such functional origins there grew a special character. And since that character is an important point of reference for the designers of new places, it is worth looking at villages in England and Scotland; and looking first at their functional origins and then at the characteristics that were derived from them.

England became, as W. G. Hoskins has pointed out,[2] a land of villages in the twenty generations from A.D. 450 to the Norman Conquest. The clearing of woodlands, often by burning, gave rise to certain place-names; later came the draining of water-logged fens, marshes and estuarine flats. By the time of Domesday Book nearly every village (excepting certain industrial settlements) that we know today had come into existence.

They were, and often remain, either grouped around a central green, strung out along a single street, haphazard in arrangement, or a combination of all three. On the green is the well (for a water supply is essential for existence),

[1] J. M. Houston, *A Social Geography of Europe*, London 1963, pp. 102–7.
[2] W. G. Hoskins, *The Making of the English Landscape*, London 1955, pp. 38–60.

sometimes the church, and later the smithy and school. At the perimeter is the back lane—the cart roads and drove roads. This plan may have originally been defensive in inspiration; it formed a stockade at night. As such, it bears a resemblance to the night-time arrangements of the wagon-trains crossing to the West of America in the nineteenth century. It may explain a national taste for smallness of scale, for informality and for the enclosed plan whose centre is a plot of open green space—a taste which is revealed in the design of some of the New Towns after the Second World War.

The period of most extensive colonial development was that between Domesday Book (1086) and the Black Death in 1348. Some of the new villages accompanied the further clearance of forests. Much of the landscape of the Chilterns, for example, may derive from such clearances. In parts of Yorkshire there is a different pattern of the same date, again related to the clearance of woodland but there also related to the development of sheep farming. It was the period of the founding of the great Cistercian abbeys. There were five or six hundred monasteries in England by 1348; of these Yorkshire had 66. Some were huge; Rievaulx, for example, supported at its peak over 150 choirmonks and 500 laybrothers. They controlled vast areas of land, not only in their immediate vicinity; their arrival, from the early twelfth century, often in places entirely undeveloped, such as Fountains, began a process that by hard work transformed their surroundings into places of great beauty. It is an unwitting lack of appreciation of the monks' labour that leads people to assume that the monks knew how to choose a naturally beautiful site.

Work, the land system, and the specific situation are some of the influences; there is also the influence of administration. For that period is the period of another characteristic feature—the parish churches. With the division of the country into parishes, thousands of small churches appeared in the landscape in the late twelfth and thirteenth centuries, their spires being added to the top in the latter part of this time. In certain parts came windmills, from the end of the twelfth century. Here are the dominants of the environment—the vertical features, the obtrusive masses of more expressive building, the foci of circulation —that provide clues to knowing the place.

The emergence of an environment through the overlaying of one functional necessity upon another can be seen clearly in Scotland, where the climate encourages a severe expression of function. In Scotland as in England the influence of the monasteries was considerable; by the sixteenth century, it has been calculated, the Church owned over a third of the arable land in the country. But the characteristic settlements were different. The towns—or 'touns'—of the lowlands originally received their names from their functional origin. There are castletouns (growing around a castle, like Castleton of Braemar), kirktouns (church-towns, growing around a parish church, again commonly dating from the twelfth century), milltouns (often now called 'Milton', and consisting essentially of mill buildings), cottartouns (sometimes shortened to 'Cotton' and based on the dwellings of cottars or cottagers), occasionally 'Ha'touns' (becoming 'Hatton' and deriving from the town of the Hall), many seatowns (along the coast), and the once ubiquitous farmtowns.

The 'fermtouns' (farmtowns) were originally neither markedly centralised nor neat. They were clusters of dwellings inhabited by joint tenants, perhaps 20 of them, who jointly farmed an area of up to 400 acres on the old open-field or 'runrig' system, casting lots annually for the strips which, with the exception of those lying fallow in rotation, fell to them for that year. The houses had their own kail-yards, which separated them from each other, and their orientation could be haphazard, relating mainly to patches of dry ground and the possibility of mutual shelter. There was no common green in the centre because the common land was the rougher land for grazing, outside the arable area bounded by the head dyke.

It is because of this system that there is no long tradition in Scotland of nucleated village design. The churches, being parish churches for a widely scattered agricultural community, were not necessarily placed in a settlement; there are kirktouns with nothing but gravestones to keep the kirk company. The water supply was always important, but not necessarily central or impressive. In any case, most of these fermtouns were swept away and replaced by single farms during the enclosures of the eighteenth century.

In contrast therefore to the English villages, especially those of the southern counties, the well-organised small old settlement is rare. But there were places where the demands of the site made tight clustering essential. An obvious example is the Fishertown or Seatown, often on an underprivileged site with little space, and acquiring a distinctive form from the habit of placing houses with their gables to the sea in order to get the maximum shelter from waves and wind and rain.

In contrast yet again, in the Highland areas north and west of the Highland Line, the clan system and the crofting system were factors that did not encourage the growth of strongly nucleated settlements. The crofts each have their own small parcel of land, and the common land is further away, frequently on the lower slopes of hills, so that along the hill slopes the former limits of cultivation and of rough pasture can often be seen. The crofting township is merely an area of such crofts, with a certain administrative organisation; its fierce or desolate beauty is a memorial to generations literally forcing some value out of a hard and grudging land.

The final point to be made about the smaller rural settlements concerns the development of distinctive house types and the influence of local materials on both the buildings and the general environment. Partly dependent on the materials, there are two basic house types: the round type (which includes the 'copanna' of the Pontine marshes, the 'pallaza' of Galicia in N.W. Spain, the 'bothan' in Scotland and the 'clachan' in Ireland), and the rectangular type (in at least two forms, the long-house, and the cruck-framed house). But even these can be reduced still further to functional origins. There seem to be two fundamental functional types: the single compact house which starts by having animals and humans under one roof, and the multiple dwelling.

Such a basic function decision can influence many centuries of building shapes. Equally decisive can be the influence of local materials, their abundance or shortage, conflicting with or reinforcing the functional requirements, and encouraging the development of either single or multiple dwellings. The multiple dwelling, such as those in the Northern Hebrides, is often developed because of shortage of roofing timbers. In one outstanding example, at Alberobello in Apulia, a tradition of building a collection of square rooms crowned with conical roofs is a continuance (revived in the sixteenth century) of an ancient Greek system of roofing Tholos tombs; but it owes its origin to the shortage of timber. What has developed is a bold use of stone corbelling to create a primitive vault.

The effect of such a tradition on the landscape can hardly be overstated. For example, the available lengths of timber can be profoundly influential. The narrow houses of the Hebrides, with walls of rough stone, are influenced by the short timbers available, sometimes thrown up by the sea. The same is true of parts of Yorkshire. On the other hand, where timber was plentiful (as in

Scandinavian house types) an entirely different plan, as well as a different surface appearance, was possible.

The external effect which materials have on a settlement, on both the shape and texture of the buildings, encourages the growth of regional character. There is the influence of roofing materials—stone, slate, tiles or thatch: the influence of walling materials—granite, sandstone, limestone, clay and straw, brick and timber: or combinations of these. Some of the most distinctive materials have caused the most distinctive architecture. In Highland areas of igneous and metamorphic rocks, ashlar work may be impossible for everyday building, so that stone dressings are omitted. Granite in the north east of Scotland makes its own hard, clean demands. The bricks of the east coast are similarly influential and distinctive in colour. 'Clunch' in East Anglia is a material entirely specific to one region. And none of them was more decisive than the limestone of the Great Oolite Stone Belt, stretching from Dorset to Yorkshire, in which, because so many of the houses were built in the seventeenth century, a quite distinct and beautiful style was able to develop in minor secular building.

At this point it may be possible to draw some general conclusions. The functional origin of the English nucleated village may have left a feeling for closeness and smallness of scale that spells warmth and home to an Englishman and a kind of eccentricity to many foreigners. The parish churches and their towers and spires gave the dominants to a familiar landscape. In different ways they were some of the components of the functional landscape; and there must be other components which are taken for granted, features that because of their familiarity spell beauty or merely safety. Are there however some underlying themes in the man-made landscape that are so elemental that they influence all environmental design and are in effect the components of beauty?

It is tempting to see in the most primitive dwellings and places of work the themes, often subconscious, that have found more elaborate expression later. They present a series of opposites—on the one hand the exposed landscape, on the other the cave, the most elementary form of shelter; or again, the plain and the mountain, the forest and the river. That these elemental components play their part in creating satisfactory environments seems to me inescapable. They swing between the poles of opportunity and threat. The forest and the river become symbolic because they represent universal problems in the control of nature. The clearing of forests and the fording of rivers are in any case fundamental to the location of settlements; but they are more than functional explanations; they are archetypal images too. Few responses are more vivid than the reaction of successive ages to the idea of the forest fire.

Such contrasts of opposites are of lasting significance. The cave spells shelter, but it also spells *enclosure*; in the most primitive state it contrasts blatantly with the extrovert and open landscape. Even to more sophisticated people, the cave as a dwelling remains a focus for curiosity. And people go back to them; there were over 37,000 underground dwellings in France, Switzerland and Italy at the beginning of this century, and in Spain people sought them as a relief from nineteenth-century overcrowding. The contrast with the cave is the air and space on to which it opens; and anyone who has explored caves knows the power of the experience that this contrast provokes.

The development of environment is concerned with the gradual bringing together of these opposites. But they are always present, and are probably the basic theme in any architectural or planning work—the control and juxtaposition of enclosure and openness, to give an experience of a linked series of experiences of the two. Among major buildings, one example is the impact of entering York Minster by the South Transept and arriving below the crossing, where the interior of the central tower soars upwards, open up to its roof. Another is that of entering Mackintosh's Glasgow School of Art, where after a low and narrow hall a cramped timber stairway suddenly opens out like a lily pad into a wide and lofty exhibition space. The experience is elemental. It is the same experience as that of the beauty of rivers, the alternation between close gorge and open reach; in architecture it is the tunnel and the open chamber, the porch and the great hall. It starts at the earliest moments in the history of design; caverns are conceived in spatial hierarchies and circulation to them through the passages finds expression in the development of the theme of the labyrinth. In the whole grouping of dwellings it is important too—the street and the square, the alleyway and the court. There are psychological explanations of these functions and images, in terms of birth and love and death; it may be that in this theme there is a parallel between experiences of natural form and those of design by the manipulation of space.

That is the first theme of the functional environment: the contrast of open and closed spaces. The second is the juxtaposition of man-made objects (dwell-ings) and the landscape. The type of contrast between a made object and nature is just as elemental. It is carried into the most contrived kind of environment and is a contrast appreciated on different scales. On the largest, there is the appreciation of a city, town or village seen from a distance against the hills or along the coast; in the middle there is the deliberate introduction of green fingers or green spaces and planting and lakes into urban areas; smaller yet there are the details of urban design, the occasional trees and the fountains of sometimes deliberately 'natural' composition; still more diminutive in scale are the goldfish bowls and the cut flowers and the aspidistra.

But whatever the scale, the conflict or careful resolution between a made object and a found one, between the work of man and the work of nature, is fundamental. It is the degree of dominance of one over the other that character-ises a particular environment and therefore characterises what may be thought suitable for it.

With these two themes—the contrast of open and closed space, and the contrast of the work of Man and Nature—the functional environment may provide the background necessary for the emergence of ideas. For it is through the manipulation of these themes, however unconsciously, that the makers of the landscape have imposed their will upon the land. And something more. Once the basic needs have been met, there enters a new freedom of choice and the possibility of self-conscious design. Into or out of the two basic themes are woven other concepts or ideas which dominate the way in which the landscape is moulded. They are the material of the succeeding chapters.

This chapter concerned the reaction of Man to the demands made upon him by Nature as he creates his own environment. That reaction is simple and technical and it is not very sophisticated. The sites are given, the problems to be solved are fairly basic; and the kind of environment that emerges is a basic one also, founded on location and materials, subject to no general pattern, but revealing always the contrasts of space and enclosure and of man's work in the midst of nature. Perhaps because of this, such an environment is often the most attractive and the most memorable. Its meaning pierces deep; and it is not surprising that, looking out over Tintern Abbey, not only at a building but at a landscape moulded originally by the agriculture of a monastic community, Wordsworth could record:

'a sense sublime
Of something far more deeply interfused,
Whose dwelling is the light of setting suns,
And the round ocean and the living air,
And the blue sky, and in the mind of man.'

2 The Landscape of the Gods

There comes a point—it may even be a turning point—in the development of civilisations when people are no longer struggling to come to terms with their surroundings but are able either to go into partnership with nature or to buy it up and to create an environment that expresses an *idea*. It may express a multiplicity of ideas; it inevitably expresses a lot of aspirations. But it can be said to express *an* idea if it has a unity and coherence: which means that some central theme or intention has dominated the scene, or can be understood as dominating the scene by later generations.

We are here in the company of great architecture and planning. All architecture reveals the scale and power and integrity of its author's intentions. This is true of all architecture—the vernacular architecture of the last chapter and the self-conscious architecture of this one. But it is clearer and more significant in the case of the latter. The intentions of the former are the solving of social problems; the intentions of the latter include solving an aesthetic problem and satisfying a definite formal aspiration.

The first chapter isolated certain factors that seem to be characteristic of satisfactory landscapes of a functional kind. Essentially there were two contrasts —the contrast of enclosure and open space, and the contrast of natural and man-made. We can now go on to see how they can be seized upon and exploited to make a deliberately sacred landscape. It can be created by the manipulation of such inevitable contrasts, together with others. One such was very deliberate: the contrast of light and dark.

The Landscape of the Gods is the landscape of ancient Greece. It is convenient to look at it first because the way I have been looking at the development of small settlements would have been foreign to the Greeks responsible for major buildings. Nowadays we tend to overemphasize technical arguments—the effect of physical demands and problems on architectural and environmental form. To the Greeks of the great period of building, particularly in the fifth century B.C., technical demands were not a central problem; it is impossible to explain fully the architecture of the great temples by reference to structural and constructional developments. To the Greeks the problem was more a sculptural one, and that meant not only carving out a building but moulding it into a significant and meaningful relationship with the landscape.

'The mountains and valleys of Greece were punctuated during antiquity by hard, white forms, touched with bright colours, which stood out in geometric contrast to the shapes of the earth. These were temples of the gods.'[1] That is the first statement in a book by Vincent Scully: *The Earth, the Temple and the Gods*, on whose very imaginative analysis I shall lean heavily in the comments which follow, though I have myself visited every site discussed.

The environment created by the Greeks of the Hellenic period can be said to express an idea (or a coherent body of ideas) because, if Mr. Scully is right, they developed an eye for combinations of landscape features as expressive of particular holiness. They went further. They placed in that landscape temples and subsidiary buildings so as to complement, or sometimes to contradict, the 'meaning that was felt in the land'. Far from being placed haphazardly, as authorities have often believed, the buildings, especially those from the seventh to the fifth centuries, were consciously placed to express a spatial concept.

The difficulty in seeing this often lies for us in our inherited modes of perception. We see objects through the windows of a fixed Renaissance perspective. The Greek vision was wider. There is a theory by Constantinos Doxiadis to account for the positioning of acropolis buildings seen from the propylon of the sanctuary. The Greeks conceived the universe as circular and realised that human vision spreads across a 180° arc of that circle; buildings are set within the arc at rhythmically related intervals, based on an Ionian ten-part and a Dorian twelve-part division of the circle.

There are other theories.[2] But at this point I merely want to note that another people's *vision* can be very different; for the Greeks this vision penetrated

[1] Vincent Scully, *The Earth, the Temple and the Gods*, Yale Univ. 1962, p. 1.
[2] R. D. Martienssen, *The Idea of Space in Greek Architecture*, Johannesburg 1956.

through spaces in which the buildings were set; they saw beyond them to the total form of the landscape, so that near and far were as one and their meaning was the same.

What this meaning was, in an outward-looking but contained environment, is discussed by Mr. Scully with reference to the foundation in Crete of the Minoan culture from about 2000 B.C. onwards, particularly at Knossos, excavated and described and even partly built by Sir Arthur Evans in the happy days before archaeology became scientific. One can trace here the development of the themes of the earth as mother goddess, the labyrinth and the horns (the symbol of the active power of the earth's motherly form) from the Neolithic period. The landscape elements are the enclosed valley (the 'Natural Megaron'), a conical hill on an axis with the palace from north to south, and a double-peaked or cleft mountain further away on the same axis. Within this landscape are four constructed, complementary types of enclosure—the labyrinthine passage, the open court, the columned pavilion, and the pillared cave.

To clarify these, here are Mr. Scully's words.

'From roughly 2000 BC onward, a clearly defined pattern of landscape use can be recognized at every palace site. More than this, each palace makes use, so far as possible, of the same landscape elements. These are as follows: first, an enclosed valley of varying size in which the palace is set; I should like to call this the "Natural Megaron"; second, a gently mounded or conical hill on axis with the palace to north or south; and lastly a higher, double-peaked or cleft mountain some distance beyond the hill but on the same axis. The mountain may have other characteristics of great sculptural force, such as rounded slopes, deep gullies, or a conical or pyramidal massing itself, but the double peaks or notched cleft seem essential to it. These features create a profile which is basically that of a pair of horns, but it may sometimes also suggest raised arms or wings, the female cleft, or even, at some sites, a pair of breasts. It forms in all cases a climactic shape which has the quality of causing the observer's eye to come to rest in its cup. Though there are many overlaps in shape and probably many unguessed complexities in their meanings, still the cone would appear to have been seen as the earth's motherly form, the horns as the symbol of its active power. All the landscape elements listed above are present at Knossos, Phaistos, Mallia, and Gournia, and in each case they themselves—and this point must be stressed—are the basic architecture of the palace complex. They define its space and focus it. Within that space the constructed elements take their form and create four complementary types of enclosure. These are: the labyrinthine passage, the open court, the columned pavilion, and the pillared cave. All these forms, both the natural and the constructed, can be shown to relate to what we otherwise know of Minoan religion and its dominant goddess, so that the natural and the man-made create one ritual whole, in which man's part is defined and directed by the sculptural masses of the land and is subordinate to their rhythms.'[1]

The approach to Knossos, both from the sea to the site and on the site from the entry to its heart, is labyrinthine in movement; and this is so whether the movement is simple or ceremonial. The latter approach was from the north. After turning, a procession could come into the court and look down its long axis to a hill closing the valley, and to the split peak of Mount Jouctas in the distance—the sacred mountain where at one time Zeus was thought to be.

The axis of the propylaea runs straight to the mountain. There it can be assumed that the natural landscape itself suggested a layout for the buildings that would have some integrity with the irregular forms surrounding it. In this there is nothing surprising. Even looking at the matter very coolly, one can appreciate that it is sensible to use natural features as guide lines in the setting out of a building site. One does not have to be very spiritual to tell a workman to line a place up on that mountain; it might, after all, be the easiest thing to do. But when the theme goes on being exploited from the land to the building there seems to be another dimension too.

The movement of people entering the palace at Knossos was labyrinthine; and it led through the elements that Mr. Scully has identified. The approach led to a court, thence by the propylaea to the main columnar hall, to the next court and so on to the dark cave-like shrine of the goddess. The movement from light to dark to light to dark is part of the labyrinth that has become the myth.

The elements there found may be profoundly important psychologically. They may indeed become part of the myth because the spatial experiences they inspire are fundamental experiences for everyone. None has more overtones

[1] Scully, op. cit., p. 11.

than the experience of movement from dark to light; it is echoed in the spiritual experience of conflict and the passage from the dark night of the senses and of the soul to the wakening light of the understanding. I suspect that in architecture and planning it has a lot to do with our intuitive fascination for certain places; and that the absence of this kind of experience is a factor in the empty monotony of modern mass environments too rationally contrived.

In the Minoan example it was an expression of genius to make the landscape itself reveal such meanings by the juxtaposition of man-made buildings. It is not necessary to describe precisely what those meanings were; it was enough to manipulate space so that it was more expressive of life and power and pilgrimage than it could have been through the simple solution of immediate functional problems.

Much more dramatic and in many ways more sinister is the citadel at Mycenae. As at Knossos, it is difficult to disentangle the impressions it creates and to suggest an authentic sequence of cause and effect. The landscape is majestic in any case—the wide spread of the plain of Argos, the hills spattered with dry trees and thin animals, the ragged and horrifying gorge, the mountain peaks leering across the site, the citadel itself crowning and spilling down its own mountain. Whether it happened or not, it would be necessary to invent a tale of murder and revenge to suit such an environment; and the horror of the return from Troy, of Agamemnon's and Clytemnestra's deaths, and of the pursuit, seems wholly in character. It is not surprising that Mr. Scully sees Mycenae as the symbol of power and dread. Its site is where the kings tried to take over from the gods.

But whatever the case, the relationship of buildings and land is close and deliberate. If at Knossos we could witness the theme of enclosure and open space and of the movement from darkness to light, here the contrast between Man and Nature is awesome and vivid. And if, as was essential, the kings of the house of Atreus were to dominate the land, the citadel and town had in themselves to make a sharper geometry out of the natural landscape—to fashion it into a new and menacing whole.

The citadel dominates and controls the pass into the plain of Argos from the north and a secondary pass to the east. The citadel is above, the town below. As you approach, slowly mounting the hills and circling the lower parts of the citadel, it unwraps itself. The individual buildings seem to punch home the

1. Wasdale Head, Cumberland: lines of settlement (p. 18)

2. Arnol, Lewis (*above*) and Pitminster, Somerset (*lower right*): dispersed and nucleated settlements contraste
   (p. 19)

British Travel Association

3.
Finchingfield, Essex:
an English village
around a green
(p. 20–21)

4. Scoraig, Ross and Cromarty: a crofting township (p. 23)

5. Nether Dallachy, Moray: a Scottish farmtown (pp. 21–22)

6. Alberobello, Apulia, Italy: group of trulli (p. 23)

7.
Knossos, Crete:
Palace of Minos
(pp. 30–31)

Mansell Collection

8.
Mycenae, Greece:
the citadel and the
Lion Gate
(pp. 32–33)

F. Mella

9. Delphi, Greece (pp. 33–34)

A. F. Kerstin

10. Epidauros, Greece (pp. 34–35)

A. F. Kerstin

11. Athens: Propylaia, Acropolis (pp. 36–37)

lesson of the site. The Treasury of Atreus (once known as the Tomb of Agamem-non, a visually appropriate designation) cuts into an artificial mound on the left. It is the ultimate enclosure. The tomb of Clytemnestra is similar, but cut out of the rising slope on the outer side as the citadel rises. The Lion Gate, its huge triangular head reflecting as a solid the gaping triangular hole in the same position in the tomb and treasury, is an artificial cutting screened by walls on the side of the hill. So its total form—a cutting, a gate and a triangular headstone— is the man-made mirror of an artificially 'natural' setting for the tombs. The living take over from the dead. Behind the Gate, Mount Zara looms up directly, the same inevitable landscape feature; looking back through the Gate the land is enclosed in the far distance by a notched hill, the other inevitable feature; looking down just below the Gate and to one side of it, the grave circle (outside the original citadel but within the later one), with its ring of standing flat stones, has a significant position for ceremony and for cult; the ancestors are laid neatly at the door between past and future.

Then you can climb up to the megaron and the throne room and the temple. From bastions such as that of the House of Columns you look down the gorge at the subject valley; from the postern gate over towards the east end of the citadel, with its secret cistern for essential water, you can look out from cover to the east and the north, at the other slopes. At the very top is the remains of the palace, and the remains of the foundations of what may have been a temple of Athena. Perhaps, even when the fortress was complete, its owner could look out from a flat roof as you look out from the platform now, surveying the land, open and supreme, feeling, in Mr. Scully's words, a 'rush of brutally triumphant exultation'. The environment of the fifteenth to the thirteenth centuries B.C. becomes immediate, and the palace founded by Perseus is terribly alive.

In a different way the theme can be picked up again some centuries later, in a landscape that determined a shrine and proclaimed the idea of conflict between men and gods. It is the sanctuary of Apollo at Delphi, laid into the lower slopes of Parnassos.

The landscape itself, massively carved and altering under changes of light, is thick with mystery; and it seems that the principal buildings—the temples of Athena and Apollo, the treasuries and the tholos—are deliberately placed to take advantage of the peaks across the valley and the succession of opening views that manifest themselves to the visitor on his approach. The tholos, dating from the end of the fifth century, is on the road from Athens that was Apollo's own first route to the site. It contained the sacred tree. It is at the point where the pilgrim coming by land first saw Apollo's shrine; and it could hardly command a more dramatic view across to the cleft that leads to the plains. Man here is small and nature is extravagantly large.

From there, Parnassos dominates more and more and the Castalian Spring gushes down. The entrance to the sanctuary was at the south-east corner; the pilgrim followed the Sacred Way past the treasuries that punctuated it.

As he entered the sanctuary the building forms began to dominate, blocking views and creating their own expressive spaces. And when the traveller at last worked his passage up the Labyrinthine Way, past the famous polygonal wall which forms a base for the temple platform, and reached the temple of Apollo, clear and proud against the hills, he could experience (as Mr. Scully suggests) a moment of 'calculated triumph and release'. He could go higher, to the theatre, and then to the stadium, lined with seats in later Roman times. But the theatre, if he paused there, is an echo of the landscape itself, hollowed into its shapes; and there he could watch the drama that developed from the choruses of Dionysos, who roamed the hills and took over the shrine for three months of every year. And looking down from its upper banks, listening to the magical acoustics set off by a single voice, he could experience—as I have done, in the rapid sunset—a quite inexpressible sense of the movement and stillness of time and the total unity of the land.

Perhaps because man was small, he was also notorious at Delphi for being unpleasant. Sacred shrines in any age have always attracted an unfair proportion of the rogues and sharks who profit materially from religion. In a quite different way he was at his less attractive at Epidauros, the major shrine of Asklepios the healer and a hospital and spa on a vast scale. But Asklepios was the son of Apollo, and it seems fair to move from Delphi and its oracle to Epidauros and its cure. The cult of Asklepios was at a peak from the fifth century B.C. onwards; as at Delphi the theatre is there; the two sites, different in many ways, have nevertheless a lot in common.

The same landscape features can be found—the mounds and cones, the peak rising between two rounded hills. Here, unlike Delphi, the main part of the site is relatively flat, a huge bowl surrounded and protected by the hills. In this site, the Temple of Asklepios is central. It opens up generously to the west, is stopped by the mountain peak to the east which crowns the buildings centrally, and rises to the theatre to the south.

Amidst the low lying ruins today it is still possible to visualise the complex of building forms which was more or less complete by the end of the fourth century. It is necessary to overcome the impression of solitariness; the place was after all thick with people, many of them sick, sleeping in the colonnades or in buildings which have entirely disappeared. It was a regional hospital.

The centre is like a low platform. Immediately above the Temple is the peak; looking diametrically the other way the land is open, but a large hill rises in the distance. This axis, the peak on one side and the hill on the other, establishes the position for Asklepios' shrine, and is a convincing example of the exploitation of landscape features by the Greek designers. In its time the view may have been interrupted by the roof and form of the tholos. Doric columns on the outer ring, Corinthian with their leaves within them, it expressed, as did the tholos at Delphi, the trees imprisoned in the architecture, or Apollo growing in the darkness—darkness imprisoned in light. In its basement may have been the sacred snakes, the symbol of the healer and the means whereby Asklepios worked his cures.

To the south, straddling the road that now leads into the site, were the appurtenances of the hospital—the guest house, bath, gymnasium, and the stadium. The stadium itself is lined up directly on a hill to the west. From this side the visitor entered the site through a propylon, between the temples of Artemis and Themis, and came out into the view to the north.

But that view is most powerful from the theatre, laid like that at Delphi into the side of the hill. Here 17,000 people could form the audience in tribute to Dionysos, all hearing perfectly the performances of the actors. Ahead to the north the land spreads out and away, giving you a momentary feeling of magnificence. The division in the hills marks where the route to the theatre and shrine comes from the old town and harbour of Epidauros, from which you can still come for a performance today. I have made the journey for a performance of *Oedipus Rex*. As the sun goes down and the crowds gather, and as later the play draws towards its frightening climax, the intentions of the planners of the site are brought home in the words, and man is consciously subjected to the power of the gods.

To see man in his grander moments, still deep in contrivance, we must look at Athens: first, at the immensely influential grouping of the Acropolis in the Periclean age in the middle of the fifth century. I do not propose to discuss in detail the orientation of the buildings, for which there are many conflicting theories that take advantage of the mathematical refinements of Greek architectural design. In general terms, we can again pick up the theme. The Acropolis itself is naturally significant, its fierce eastern cliffs facing towards the cone of Lycabettos, its approachable western end looking back past the Pnyx towards Salamis, the site of the great sea victory by Themistocles in 480 B.C. that set Athens on its eminence. Within the space of the Acropolis the buildings achieve a remarkable effect. They are insular and outward looking; they are self-contained monuments in space; and yet they combine forces to produce a movement and changing series of dominants that make another magic—there takes place between them what has been described as 'crashes of unison'.

The Acropolis is a limestone mass, and the buildings of Pentelic marble give emphasis to its form. Thus the Parthenon, started in 452 B.C., dominates the entire scene from any view. As the Panathenaic procession moved through the Agora and up the hill to its western end with the Areopagus on the right, the Parthenon disappeared from view and appeared again as the dominant it was meant to be.

In this, and in the layout on the top of the hill, the theme of using the landscape as a determinant of building form is clear again. The Doric Parthenon is massive, masculine and propulsive, incapable of being apprehended at a single point. More gentle and humane, the Ionic Erechtheion is placed, a later building, to make a meaning of the area as a whole. A combination itself of several different shrines, it is subtle, clear and assymetrical. Between them the space is empty, but it is a space once punctuated by the statue of Gaia and the altar of Athena. Looking outwards, it is suddenly clear how Lycabettos, away to one side and distinctive in outline, is part of this space and a dominant that plays a significant part in a three-dimensional unity on the bare rock. There are axes in space, positive and negative forms, solids and voids; and all the time Lycabettos provides a fixed point of reference. From its slopes looking back, the Acropolis too is distinctive; Lycabettos is an essential feature in the understanding of the Acropolis.

But if there is one building more than any other which displays the excitement of manipulated space, it is the Propylaia. The axis of the Propylaia faces directly towards Salamis, so that the whole group and its entry is deliberately lined up on the place where the Persians were finally beaten off in one of the decisive battles of the world. This seems convincing as a key to the planning; though it is only fair to point out that if you follow the axis that runs through the Parthenon in the other direction, it takes you straight to the Hilton Hotel.

The Propylaia group is the entrance, approached by steps or perhaps by ramps, and its great wings reach forward at each side so that a person is drawn in and through it, involved in its columned spaces, and at the same time held back by its outward looking grandeur. On one side the temple of Nike Apteros punctuates the sky, and is also a positive form by the same architect as the Propylaia, Mnesicles, emphasising the view out to Salamis. The entrance is a perfect balance of forces; between enclosure and openness, between solidity and the penetration of air. It is a deliberate exploitation of the illusion of space, the inter-penetration of exterior and interior, and of continuity with the moulded space of the city. As such it is one of architecture's most expressive symbols, and it draws to itself many of the known themes of environmental design.

These were sacred sites; there are similarities in secular ones. The Greeks drew no hard line of design between religious and secular buildings, and we can see in the city as a whole—and in the agora in particular—the extension of some of the ideas I have just discussed.

The agora lies, in Athens and elsewhere, below the citadel, on the lower ground. It is the place of gathering, which means far more than merely the market-place; it could contain, in addition to the stoas or colonnades (used for all kinds of purposes), the bouleuterion (council house) and the prytaneion (town hall). It is the place of the people, and the history of Greek city planning is partly the story of the decline of the acropolis and the progressive development of the agora as the real heart of the community, the central zone of the city.[1]

Aristotle remarked that an acropolis is suitable for oligarchy and monarchy, level ground for democracy. The level ground became the centre of trade and politics as democracy grew; it was the meeting place for chatter and discussion, for Socrates among the booths, and for the growth of a philosophical speculation that saw through the unethical pretensions of the old gods and influenced the rationalisation of the environment.

The agora is surrounded loosely by houses that form an undistinguished

[1] R. E. Wycherley, *How the Greeks built Cities*, London 1948, Chapter IV, pp. 50–86.

background. But this part of the city was also conceived (or, in the earlier cases, grew) as a series of spaces related to the city and to the landscape as a whole.

The characteristic feature of Hellenistic planning was the *stoa*. Athens has the Stoa of Attalos, dating from the second century B.C. and entirely reconstructed by American archaeologists a few years ago. It is a technique for regularising the space of the agora and containing within a definite colonnaded form the units or spaces that served various mercantile purposes. It is both cave and grove—and so is the city.

The city is not planned axially, it does not find its generating lines in streets, there is no hierarchy of major and minor roads. That kind of planning was a later Roman development (a kind of half-way stage can be seen in the essentially Hellenistic planning of Pompeii). Nor is it a contained city, finding its shapes and streets dictated by surrounding city walls; that development was first Roman and then especially mediaeval. The walls of the Greek city were loosely flung around it, following the defensive contours of the land and hardly related to the houses and alleyways within. As such the city was a three-dimensional set of related volumes, the biggest volumes reaching out to the bays and hills that characterise the Greek landscape.

This is very clear in the cases of deliberate Greek city planning on new or rebuilt sites.[1] Miletus in Ionia was refounded to an ideal plan after its destruction by the Persians and their subsequent defeat in 479 B.C. The planner may have been Hippodamus, who was a Milesian and certainly planned Piraeus some years later. Miletus is, in any case, the original for the Hippodamian grid. The agora lies on the low ground, the residential blocks are distributed on either side. There is an even carpet of residential blocks, laid over the ground as a spatial unit and ending without terminals where the site demands.

At Priene, refounded at the end of the fourth century, beneath a towering hill, there is the perfect expression of this plan. Again the streets come to their natural open ends; the wall is irregularly built around the area, including the possibly unused heights. The city is outward looking to its territory. It is part of nature, but there is now a resolved conflict with it. The rational plan is laid on the contours as though they were all flat, and because the ground slopes there is a notable clash between man's reason and organisation and the demands of

[1] Ibid, Chapter II, pp. 15–35.

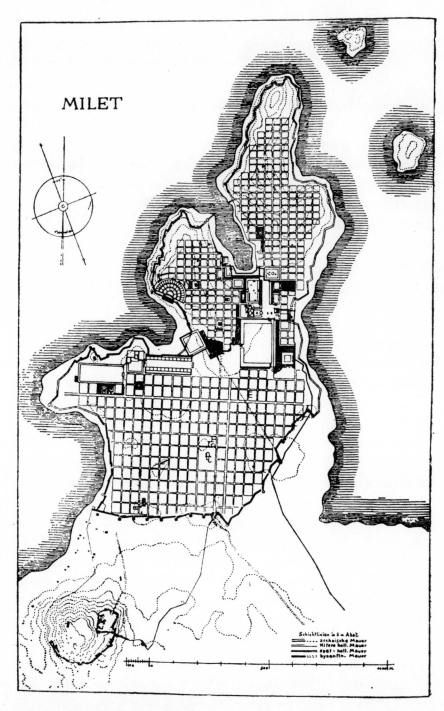

MILET

Miletus: plan of the city (see p. 38)

natural forms. It may not be surprising that this should happen at a time of intense intellectual activity; we shall see (in a later chapter) the same contrast of plan and site taking place in the neoclassic planning of the Enlightenment.

For the moment, however, we can see the manner in which natural, given phenomena could be used and manipulated by planners as determinants of the environment, forcing a unity of a mysterious kind on the buildings within it.

The theme of this chapter is that it is not necessary to impose arbitrary concepts upon the man-made environment, as some neoclassic and later formal planners have tried to do. The ideas are waiting there already. But it *is* necessary consciously to exploit them. Without that the resulting environment is merely disorganised, and perhaps even expresses the failure of the human mind to make its contribution to the environment offered by nature. The environment is man and nature in *antis*, so to speak—or man and nature unified.

And this is the Landscape of the Gods, because it is where man recognises the power of the gods and subordinates himself to it. We could find contemporary phrases for this; I have used more romantic ones because of the romance of the ancient sites. The sacred landscape is thus not the obvious explicit one, such as a graveyard surrounding a church, but the landscape in which the degree of collaboration between natural forms and conscious design is most marked.

Its components are those found, but not yet fully developed, in natural landscapes (whatever they are) or simpler functional ones. They are the contrasts of open and closed space, of man-made and natural, and of light and darkness. We have seen, without worrying overmuch about the peculiar characteristics of the Gods themselves, how these contrasts can be found in certain ancient Greek sites. At Knossos, at Mycenae, at Delphi, at Epidauros, at Athens, all of these contrasts can be discovered; and all of them contribute to the well-known emotive effect that the sites have on the visitor and certainly had on people in antiquity.

There are probably still more such contrasts in the continuing dialetic of perception and thought. Perhaps another is the contrast of stillness and movement, which we have seen at Mycenae and Delphi, and which is probably a key component of good architectural design. Perhaps another again is the contrast of dry and wet, like the contrast of light and dark.

Certainly the Greeks, in their stories as well as their buildings, saw the power of the sea and of streams in relation to the harder forms of the land, and the symbolic significance of the sea journey as a spiritual pilgrimage. To the seaman on the Aegean approaching Attica, the promontory of Cape Sounion must have spelled some kind of completion; there stood dramatically the Temple of Poseidon, always memorable to voyagers. And from it, looking out towards the islands in the west, there develops again that sense of mystery and of inevitability created not just by the islands themselves but by the act of someone in identifying the place to see it from and providing the rational framework of buildings at that very place.

> 'The river is within us, the sea is all about us;
> The sea is the land's edge also, the granite
> Into which it reaches, the beaches where it tosses
> It hints of earlier and other creation:
> The starfish, the horseshoe crab, the whale's backbone;
> The pools where it offers to our curiosity
> The more delicate algae and the sea anemone.
> It tosses up our losses, the torn seine,
> The shattered lobsterpot, the broken oar
> And the gear of foreign dead men. The sea has many voices,
> Many gods and many voices.'[1]

[1] T. S. Eliot, *The Dry Salvages*, from *The Four Quartets*, London 1944.

3 The Metaphysics of Light

In 1144 the new abbey church of Saint-Denis was consecrated. It was a major event for its time. It was also a major event in architectural history. Its author was Abbot Suger, one of the decisive figures of the early Middle Ages. Churchman, scholar, administrator, politician, adviser to king and Pope, he worked during the period of his administration to make Saint-Denis a central symbol of the unity of the state and of the church; he used the opportunity of rebuilding the church to make that building a symbol of Heaven. In doing so he became in effect the father of the Gothic, of an architectural synthesis complete and coherent in its details, and capable of inspiring a vision of ultimate truth and reality.

That such a description is not merely the fancy of enthusiasts of later generations can be confirmed from Suger's own words. For Suger, unlike most of his contemporaries and immediate successors, not only supervised the operation, but left a record of his intentions and of the work that went into their realisation. His two manuscripts—the *Booklet on the Consecration of the Church of Saint-Denis* and his *Report on the Administration*—state clearly the ideals that were in his mind, developed and refined as the building proceeded.

'Thus when—out of my delight in the beauty of the house of God—the loveliness of the many-coloured gems has called me away from external cares, and worthy meditation has induced me to reflect, transferring that which is material to that which is immaterial, on the diversity of sacred virtue; then it seems to me that I see myself dwelling, as it were, in some strange region of the universe which neither exists entirely in the slime of the earth nor entirely in the purity of Heaven; and that, by the grace of God, I can be transported from this inferior to that higher world in an anagogical manner.'[1]

Throughout the process of erecting the abbey church, Suger was not merely concerned with the development of an architectural technique. He was concerned with a vision, with an ultimate meaning that his architecture could convey—with, in other words, its metaphysics. And in that architecture the most significant component was light.

Suger was infatuated with light. Light was more than an element made capable of exploitation by the structural developments of the Gothic style. Light was a medium expressive in itself, a medium out of which the architecture could be composed. As such, the manipulation of light was not merely a characteristic of Gothic; it was a basic constituent.

It was capable of control and exploitation because to the architect was presented at the right moment the fact and the potential of stained glass. It was not new. But it travelled with extraordinary rapidity through the eleventh century to its technical fulfilment in the twelfth century and its full-scale use in the thirteenth. And it had all the greater significance and effect because it was more than the plaything of architects. It had, in keeping with the Gothic style of which it was such a crucial part, a respectable background in the philosophical thought of the time. This is known as the 'light metaphysic'.

Within the last two decades a lot of new light has been thrown upon the Gothic style through historical research and publication. It seems to me that certain basic themes emerge:

1. That architecture and stained glass—or space and light—are indivisible; and that the unity between them in the high Gothic period was possible because there existed a general and fundamental *idea* of the cathedral.
2. That a major element in this idea was explicitly contained in some of the prevailing philosophical ideas of the time.
3. That it was carried into effect consistently by certain architects, in architectural terms and in accordance with the way in which an architect thinks.

But how does an architect think? In order to answer this it is necessary to look at the processes of his thought, at the general background—the landscape of ideas in which he lives—and the pressures upon him to think in certain patterns, dictated by the thought processes of his time. As it happens, the period

[1] Abbot Suger, *Report on the Administration* (trans. Panofsky), quoted in Johnson, *Radiance of Chartres*, p. 24.

is one for which such an attempt is possible. It was not only intellectually one of the most exciting periods in history; there existed an extraordinary correlation between activities and thought.

'The great revival', says David Knowles, 'of the eleventh century, which gathered amplitude and momentum in the twelfth century, and reaches its highest and most characteristic, though not perhaps its most universal, achievement in the thirteenth century, was manifest in all contemporary mental activities and affected theology, philosophy, religious reform, both private and public, literature as well in poetry as in prose, architecture, sculpture, illumination, law both canon and civil, mathematics and the natural sciences.'[1] This achievement found its architectural expression in the cathedral.

Increasingly, as its plan form was refined, its function developed, its possibilities explored, the cathedral came to be seen, not only as the church of the diocese and the seat of the bishop, not only as the principal centre for the performance of the solemn liturgy and the administration of religious affairs, but as being in itself an image of the celestial city. 'How awesome is this place. Truly this is the house of God and the gate of Heaven, and it shall be called the court of the Lord'; the sentiment formed part of the liturgy, and was sung at the consecration of a church.

In recognising it as such we have perhaps been unduly influenced in looking at the cathedral as a didactic work. In his superb study of *Religious Art in France in the Thirteenth Century*,[2] Emile Male showed in detail over fifty years ago how the church was virtually a manual of instruction; its windows and statues could bring directly in visible form the matter of history and of doctrine to people unable to read. It was the Bible of the Poor; it was, as Victor Hugo had described it, a book of stone. An elaborate iconography was worked out. But this was to look upon the cathedral at only one level—the level of explicit teaching. The windows, for example, told a story or made a point through their representational content. In doing so they were doing in a rather bright way what a picture or a statue could do also, carrying out in a more sophisticated medium what the Romanesque church had to paint on its walls.

If this were the whole story we could continue to look at the windows as pictures, and their exploitation as a historical accident. But if, as *the medium for*

1 David Knowles, *The Evolution of Mediaeval Thought*, London 1962, p. 79.
2 Now published under the title of *The Gothic Image*, London 1961.

the introduction of light, they are regarded as architectural elements, they have a message which is more profound, and which is that of the idea of the cathedral as a whole.

The book which in recent years has given the most thorough and fluent account of this idea is Otto von Simson's *The Gothic Cathedral*.[1] In an exhaustive account of the work of Suger at Saint-Denis and of the rebuilding of Chartres, first of the west façade after the fire of 1134 and later of the remainder of the cathedral after the disastrous fire of 1194, von Simson expounds the thesis of Gothic architecture as 'an image, more precisely, as the representation of super-natural reality'. The mediaeval sanctuary was the image of Heaven.

It is reasonable to suppose that what Suger realised he could do in the rebuilding of the sanctuary of Saint-Denis the builders of Chartres and others saw they could do with the whole edifice. Not only might the sanctuary itself be an image of Heaven, the repository of the Divine Presence. The entire cathedral, developed into a complex unity, could be an image too. But as such an image it demanded a very special perfection.

The celestial city, the house of God, demanded an organisation of its parts that would make it *in itself* an image of unity and consistency, and one that could be experienced by the faithful. The building itself could reveal something supernatural; it was itself literally a *revelation*. And it revealed the ultimate reality by analogy. The cathedral, in whole and in part, and in the relationship between them, was an architectural analogy of God.

Starting from an entirely different viewpoint, the great historian of Gothic, Paul Frankl, in his last work *Gothic Architecture* came to a similar conclusion about the roots of Gothic. At the close of that book, which starts with the unemotional statement, 'The Gothic style evolved from within Romanesque church architecture when diagonal ribs were added to the groin-vault', Frankl comes round to pointing out that ultimately this is an insufficient explanation; we have to seek instead for its spiritual aim and sense of direction; and the ultimate root of the Gothic is none other than Jesus of Nazareth. 'Christianity, which was born out of Jesus, as the Christ, had its own immanence, of which the organisation of the Church—first its institutions and later its architecture— were a branch. It is in this context that the Gothic style should be understood:

[1] Otto von Simson, *The Gothic Cathedral*, first published 1956; references from the second edition, London 1962.

it accompanied one stage in the development of Christianity.'[1] It was characteristic of that stage that the architecture should reveal those roots and should make manifest the truth and the splendour of the Godhead.

Now making things manifest—*manifestatio*—was, as Panofsky has shown, one of the fundamental aims of scholastic thought. The principle of 'clarification for clarification's sake' can be applied not only to the direction and scope of their thinking, and to their processes of exposition, but also to their architecture.[2] If therefore there was a definite idea of the cathedral, if it was an image which could reveal reality, and if that reality could be made manifest through the medium of the architecture, we must ask what were the means employed by the cathedral designers to achieve their purpose. *How* does the Gothic cathedral inspire this religious and metaphysical experience? It does so, according to the analysis by von Simson, by means of two things—*Measure* and *Light*.

There seems little doubt of the constant importance attached by the cathedral builders to the use of mathematics. But the same background of thinking that attached such importance to number also attached importance to light. And it is on light, the second means whereby the architect could give actuality to his vision, that I want to concentrate.

The mediaeval theory of the *light-metaphysic* finds its origin in neo-Platonism —in the 'doctrine of Ideas or Forms, which asserted that the individuals and their qualities in the visible world were only appearances, reflections of or approximations to the real exemplar or Form in the realms of reality, which Form was comprehensible only by a perfected intelligence.'[3] The object of knowledge was the external unities that lay behind the world of visible things. It is easy to see how this could lead to a method of explanation in the Christian era, an explanation of the differences between the spiritual and the material. All reality in the end was spiritual reality, and visible things were an approximation to it.

St. Augustine (354–430), transforming this basic concept into one of the most influential bodies of writing in the Christian era, saw in it the relevance of light. 'For him . . .', says Knowles, 'Light is the one intellectualizing element in the whole of creation, reflecting the uncreated light of God. In man it is the

[1] Paul Frankl, *Gothic Architecture*, Pelican History of Art, London 1962, pp. 266–8.
[2] Panofsky, *Gothic Architecture and Scholasticism*, London 1957, p. 35.
[3] Knowles, op. cit., p. 7.

illumination of the Word; in the sensible world . . . it is the created light of the sun, and in things inanimate it is the number which is, as it were, a light immanent in things.'[1] The soul grasped the Ideas by illumination—in the words of another writer, 'an inner light which enabled the souls to recognise them. In the *City of God* (he) referred to this incorporeal light as the means by which the soul reaches sure knowledge. Elsewhere he shows how all truth and understanding are part of the divine light, with God our master'.[2]

The notion was given further importance by its use by the pseudo-Denis, the Syrian monk of the early sixth century, who gave his identity as that of St. Paul's disciple, Dionysius the Areopagite, and thus ensured for his works (whose authorship was not questioned until the fifteenth century) considerable respect and authority. It appears in the neo-Platonic School of Chartres, the centre of humane studies in Europe throughout the twelfth century. It reaches its fullest expression in the work of Robert Grosseteste, the Chancellor of Oxford University and Bishop of Lincoln (1175–1253).

Grosseteste was a major figure in the study of the natural sciences and of experimental science. He recognised the basic importance of mathematics as a means of description and understanding of the visible world, and taught the use of observation and experiment. To him there was no final gulf between metaphysics and physics; the study of mathematics, physics, geometry, optics and astronomy were part of the philosopher's task.

Possibly between 1215 and 1220 he wrote *De Luce* and *De Motu Corporali et Luce* and expounded his 'Light metaphysics' in these and later works. To him the intelligence is, as Augustine had urged, illumined by a spiritual light which is from God. This spiritual *lux* has an analogy in the corporeal *lux*, whose mathematical laws underlie the operations of physical things. To him the study of geometrical optics is the key to the knowledge of the natural world; and phenomena seen therein can be used as an analogy for supernatural truths. The operation of Divine Grace, for example, through the free-will, is like light shining through coloured glass.[3]

[1] Ibid., p. 49.
[2] G. Leff, *Mediaeval Thought*, London 1958, p. 41.
[3] For a full account of Grosseteste's scientific writing see A. C. Crombie, *Robert Grosseteste and the Origins of Experimental Science*, Oxford 1953. Translation of *De Luce* by C. C. Riedl, Milwaukee 1942.

How this kind of analogy is justified is demonstrated, for example, in his comments on the knowledge of *Truth*.

'Created truth too, therefore, shows that which is, but not in its own illumination (lumen), but in the light (lux) of the supreme truth, as colour shows body, but only in the light spread upon it. Nor is this an insufficiency of light, that it reveals body through colour, since colour itself is not a shining light added to a superfused light; but the power of light is this, that light does not obscure colour which lights up beyond itself, but, on the other hand, it does not illumine that which lights up beyond itself. In the same fashion is the power of the light of the supreme truth, which so illumines the created truth that, illumined itself, it reveals the true object. Consequently, the light of the supreme truth is not to other truths as the sun is to other luminaries of the sky, which it obscures in its brightness, but rather as the sun to colours which it illumines. The light alone, therefore, of the supreme truth shows first and through itself that which is, as light alone shows bodies. But by this light the truth of the thing, too, shows that which is, as colour shows bodies by the light of the sun. It is true, therefore, as Augustine testifies, that no truth is perceived except in the light of supreme truth. But, as the weak eyes of the body do not see coloured bodies, unless the light of the sun is spread upon them, but are not able to look upon the very light of the sun in itself, except only as it is spread upon coloured bodies, so too the weak eyes of the mind do not look upon true things themselves except in the light of the supreme truth; but they are not able to look on the supreme truth itself in itself, but only in a kind of conjunction and superfusion in the true things themselves.'[1]

But if light can provide this metaphysical analogy, it is also in its natural form of the utmost significance. In visible light the powers of divine light were most plainly manifested; and so the study of optics was the basis of natural explanation. He discussed in detail problems of vision, properties of mirrors and lenses; and there are fascinating passages in his explanations of the properties of visual rays, of refraction, and in his explanation of the rainbow—a phenomenon which seems to have preoccupied many mediaeval scholars. Colour was 'light incorporated with the transparent medium'. One particular aspect of his views on perception seems immediately relevant. He believed in the existence of both

[1] From Grosseteste *On Truth*. McKeon, *Selections from Mediaeval Philosophers*, New York 1929, Vol. I, pp. 273–4.

12. Cape Sounion: Temple of Poseidon
    (p. 41)

13. Athens: Agora and Stoa of Attalos
    (pp. 37–38)

14. Chartres Cathedral: views from the south east and the north west (Chapter 3)

15. Canterbury Cathedral: Trinity Chapel (pp. 55 *et seq.*)

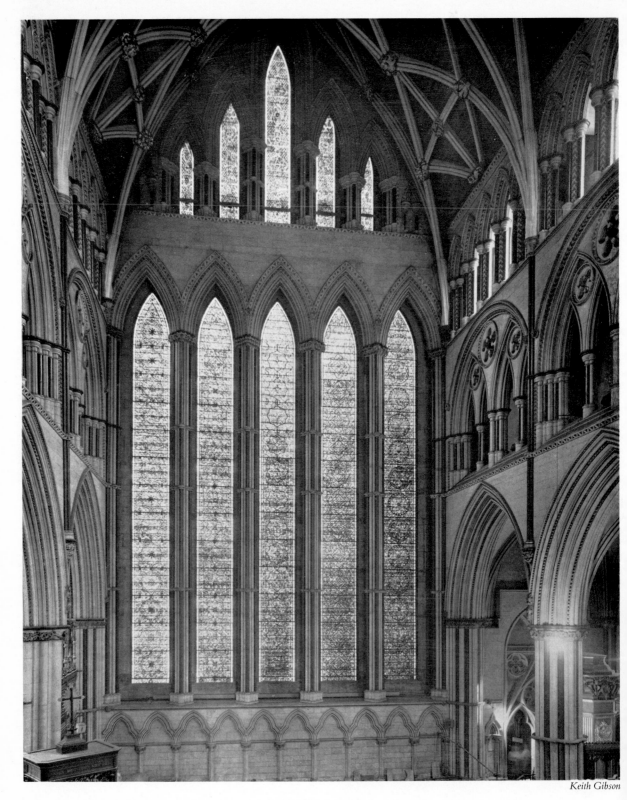

16. York Minster: North Transept and Five Sisters Window (p. 55)

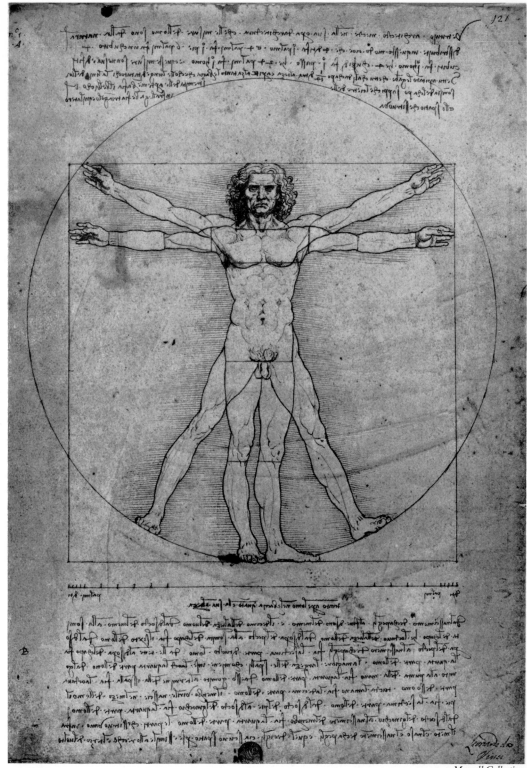

17. Vitruvian Man (Leonardo da Vinci) (p. 63)

18. Villa Capra (Rotonda) Vicenza (p. 64)

Aerofilms Ltd

19. Palma Nuova, Italy (p. 66)

20.
Rome: Piazza del
Popolo (pp. 66–67)

A. F. Kersting

The French Government Tourist Office

21. The Palace of Versailles (p. 68)

intramitted and extramitted vision. That is, he accepted the ancient Greek view (based on his knowledge of Euclid's *Optics*) that visual rays go out from the eye, so that the figure contained by them is a cone with its vertex in the eye and its base the field of vision; but he believed that some rays were received by the eye as well. His follower and pupil, Roger Bacon, co-ordinated these by the explanation that an immaterial visual species went forth from the eye and gave rise to sight, while material light rays entered the eye.[1]

We have here a coherent and influential philosophical theory, in which light has both a metaphysical power and a natural significance. If therefore a scholastic involved in the conception of the cathedral as the image of heaven required an intellectual justification, he had available for his proposals a splendid theoretical explanation of the meaning of light. But it is one thing to describe a theory that happened to be current at the same time as some buildings were being erected; it is quite another to prove that there is a genuine relation of cause-and-effect between them, and still another to indicate the results in the actual buildings.

There can be no doubt, for example at Chartres, of the familiarity of such ideas to the people commissioning cathedrals; for at Chartres, the School was at its height throughout the twelfth century. It was the home of neo-Platonism. It had international fame and its scholars were some of the luminaries of their age. Adelard of Bath, Bernard of Chartres, his brother Thierry, Gilbert de la Porrée, William of Conches were outstanding writers. And the man who was described as in his time the central figure of English learning, John of Salisbury, ended his days in 1180 as Bishop of the diocese. The school was responsible for some of the main translations from the ancient philosophers; it was well known for its study of mathematics and natural science; it was a place to which scholars came from all over Europe. And during the time of its pre-eminence was built the most self-consciously considered cathedral, a work considered of prime national importance, for which vast sums were subscribed and for which people gathered from many sources. It is reasonable to suppose that even the most academic scholar must have noticed that there was a cathedral going up on his doorstep; and that even the most mundane craftsman must have been aware of the existence of a school of thought. In fact, the two worlds were by no means separate; and we can even see a direct connection between the famous simile of

[1] Crombie, op. cit., p. 114 note.

Bernard of Chartres of the moderns as dwarfs who can see further than the giants, the ancients on whose shoulders they are perched, and the famous windows in the cathedral of the four prophets of the Old Testament bearing on their shoulders the four evangelists of the New.

The acquiring of a discipline of mind—the ability to recognise principles and to see their relevance to applications—does argue at least an awareness of other fields of activity. And perhaps more than an awareness. Although architecture is to some degree autonomous, its methods are dependent upon other disciplines and the progress of those disciplines. An architect cannot push his skill a stage further without a recognition and basic understanding of what science, history, and art have to offer.

If this is so, then any designer must be in some way influenced in his approach by the current ideas of his time, and perhaps more by the methods implied by those ideas. I believe this happens even though—or even because—the architect himself may not be able precisely to explain what those ideas are or how his own work embodies them. They must be there implicitly, actually built in, in the terms of his own discipline.

An architect's work can therefore never be properly explained without reference to the 'landscape of ideas' in which he lives, the intellectual environment which opens up and limits the directions he can take in his own thought and imagination. He may not bother to analyse that environment; but if he is any sort of creative force at all he must inevitably be the recipient of ideas that are in common circulation. And if he himself cannot see it, the historian is obliged to seek out just how those ideas were effective in directing his approach.

In the twelfth and thirteenth centuries we can establish in a remarkable way the connection between the architectural process and those of philosophical and general thought. In one respect it has been done by Panofsky, in his lecture on *Gothic Architecture and Scholasticism*. Rightly recognising the danger of drawing naïve parallels between different branches of activity, he sees instead a genuine cause-and-effect relationship, which 'comes about by diffusion rather than by direct impact. It comes about by the spreading of what may be called, for want of a better term, a mental habit—reducing this overworked cliché to its precise Scholastic sense as a "principle that regulates the act, *principium importans ordinem ad actum*".'[1]

[1] Panofsky, op. cit., p. 20.

This mental habit, Panofsky explains, is seen in the literary field, not so much by the contents of writing, but in the *modus operandi* of the Scholastic writer; and its influence upon the architect lay in a particular method of procedure which was characteristic of the schoolman with whom he had to deal. Without following Panofsky's argument in detail, one can summarise some of its features. It was a major achievement of the early scholastic period, brought to its fullness in the *Summa* of the thirteenth century, to arrange information and arguments in a scheme of presentation that clarified the actual processes of reasoning. We accept it as natural that a work of scholarship should be arranged according to a logical scheme of presentation, of division and sub-division; and we expect to find some logic in the relationships of respective subdivisions to their divisions. But 'this kind of systematic articulation was quite unknown until the advent of Scholasticism'. Consistently pursued, it led to what Panofsky calls the 'postulate of clarification for clarification's sake'.[1]

Panofsky sees the carrying out of this method in the planning, the articulation, of the Gothic cathedral. He goes so far as to draw a parallel between the structure and layout of the philosophical treatise and the relationship of parts and of the parts to the whole in the architecture of the cathedral: and also between the overall concept of *manifestatio*, of clarification, and what the architect was attempting to do.

Clearly it is not difficult in pursuing this analogy to fall into the danger that Panofsky himself recognised; and of course there have not been wanting scholars to point this out and to show the inadequacies of some of the detailed arguments. But it may be that the details do not matter. It is probably essential to the argument not to take too much notice of the details; for if the basic idea is sound then it is only the basic idea which matters; and that is that in his *modus operandi* the architect was part of the scholastic process and thought in the way that thinkers of his time did. His education, after all, was, though more limited in content, carried out in the same way.

What I am arguing here is that there is abundant evidence of the architect making use in his thinking of a system; and that system is precisely the system of scholastic thinking. But even if he had never heard of a scholastic thinker, all the pressures about him at the time were towards systematisation—in thought, in institutions, in mechanical invention. The early Middle Ages were above all

[1] Ibid., pp. 32–5.

the age of making systems, of which the great systematic treatises—the Summae —were the intellectual highlights. Everyone must have seemed obsessed with putting everything in order. It was the age which saw the organisation and definition of the guilds, the founding of the Universities and their disciplines and constitutions, the codification of law, the organisation of the Feudal system. In church practice itself, it was predominantly the time when the liturgy of the church was regularised and systematised, in which the church's year was defined and fixed. It was a time when urban society grew rapidly and in which town plans—of new foundations, of burghs and bastides—were systematically devised and controlled. And it was the time when, as a result of careful precision and measurement in practical fields, invention led to the mechanisation of mining and metallurgy, to the development of power-driven machinery and the harnessing of water; in the subjects to which I have referred—Measure and Light—to the invention of the mechanical clock and of spectacles.[1]

In such a world, attempting to produce harmony and above all order in human affairs, the architect stood in the centre of human creation, creating a synthesis as the great philosophers created theirs. Indeed, as Knowles says of St. Thomas Aquinas, 'the two Summae have been compared, not inaptly, to the whole mass of the mediaeval fabric and furnishings of such a building as Salisbury cathedral, their exact contemporary.'[2]

And throughout the whole process, embedded in the whole daily structure of common thought, runs the theme of clarity and of illumination, of human as well as of divine affairs. You only have to browse among words and comments from sources of the period to encounter time and time again the constant analogy of light, as much in the explanation of ordinary phenomena as of supernatural concepts. If Suger was infatuated with light, so was his century and the following one. They were obsessed by it. In the church's own daily practice, which the faithful attended, the Mass, as Jungmann points out, was systematically organised into parts,[3] and increasing weight was given, not to the content of prayers but to the imagery of ceremonies, and to the alternation between the loud and soft tones of prayer. It was surely a parallel to the alternation between light and dark in the imagery and the building. To the faithful the full imagery

[1] cf. Crombie, op. cit., p. 18.
[2] Knowles, op. cit., p. 256.
[3] J. A. Jungmann, *Missarum Solemnia*, abridged edit. London 1959, p. 85.

of the Easter Vigil, in which with the 'exultet' the wholly darkened church is lit by the new fire and the lights lit from it come up on the declaration of God's work for men, would be immediately meaningful in a way which we have lost. And daily also; for it was at this time (about the middle of the thirteenth century) that the opening of the Gospel of St. John with its identification of Christ as the Light which cannot be quenched by the darkness, was added to the end of the Mass by the Dominican rite.

Light indeed was over all. And the architect was involved in it as a medium as much as was the mystic. In his more mundane way, his soul may have responded to that of an anonymous Cistercian monk of the thirteenth century who concluded his study of *The Seven Pillars of Wisdom* with this comment on the soul: 'Delighting thus constantly in the love of God, the soul will often find itself poured out in an ecstasy of love. It is rapt from all thought of present and earthly things. It is stupefied by the beauty of God, by the glory of the King and of his kingdom. It tastes God's sweetness and rests in His eternal quiet. Silently it dwells on the shining of Heaven's incorporeal light, the savour of being deeply filled with God and the hidden things which He reveals to the soul in His silence.'[1]

We do not, of course, find such sparkling descriptions of their experiences in the writings of architects or artists of the time. The business of such persons was (and is) to get on with the job. Writing was the business of the professional writer. The architects of the Middle Ages did not have the advantage—or the disadvantage—of being able to write a book after the event to make sure that people recognised the qualities of a building which might not be clear from the building itself. But it is notable that one of the few writers who made a detailed record of the technology of certain crafts, the early twelfth-century monk Theophilus, did in a brief passage make observations that respond to those of the philosophers and mystics. In his *Schedule of the divers arts* written in the early twelfth century, a flat and itemised schedule of information about certain crafts including stained glass, he writes in the Introduction to Book III, 'you have approached the House of God with confidence, and have adorned it with much beauty; you have embellished the ceilings or walls with varied work in different colours and have, in some measure, shown to beholders the paradise of God, glowing with varied flowers, verdant with herbs and foliage, and cherishing

[1] From the Domus Interior, published in *The School of Self-Knowledge*, London 1956.

with crowns of varying merit the souls of the saints. You have given them cause to praise the Creator in the creature and proclaim his wonder in his works. For the human eye is not able to consider on what work first to fix its gaze; if it behold the ceilings they glow like brocades; if it considers the walls they are a kind of paradise; if it regards the profusion of light from the windows it marvels at the inestimable beauty of the glass and the infinitely rich and various workmanship.'[1]

If then it can be inferred that the use of the cathedral as a vehicle for the promotion of a religious and mystical experience was either a conscious or unconscious intention of the early mediaeval architect and artist, and that the manipulation of light as the principal channel of this experience was central to his plan, we must now ask what evidence there is in the buildings themselves either to confirm the intention or to indicate their success in giving it reality. What is the specification for a 'paradise of God'?

To do this we must be clear as to what we would *expect* to find if the thesis is correct. We would expect to find a representation or an analogy, not only of a literal kind but one contained in the physical use of architectural elements. This is in accordance with the mediaeval attitude towards symbolism, which we have sometimes tended to interpret in too narrow a manner. The symbolic code was not only a literary one; that kind of symbol has more, in traditional church terminology, the character of a 'sign' rather than a 'symbol'. A symbol, to the mediaeval mind, could be more direct and not require an intermediate explanation. A thing might become symbolic when its own nature was so clear and so profoundly exposed that while being even more profoundly itself it gave knowledge of something, not other, but implied by its very nature. Von Simson quotes a thinker as defining 'symbolic vision' as the ability to apprehend within the objects of sense perception the invisible reality of the intelligible that lies beyond them.[2]

We are therefore looking for symbolism contained in the actual use of light and colour, without intermediate explanation—for the full potential of light in itself. And to interpret what we have seen of the significance of the 'Light Metaphysic' in terms more close and practical to the designer, we are looking

1 Theophilus, *De Diversis Artibus*, trans. C. R. Dodwell, Nelson's Mediaeval Texts 1961, Introduction to Book III.
2 Maximus the Confessor. quoted in von Simson, op. cit., pp. xix–xx.

for the use of light that corresponds with the way in which the philosopher considered it—the Divine Light that illumines and transforms the corporeal light of the visible world and the bodies known through it.

Mediaeval thinkers—not only Suger but also such as Hugh of St. Victor, founder of the so-called mystical school of St. Victor—realised that the stained glass window had this power. Just as the image was used of the contrast between the 'veiled' truth of the Old Testament and the 'unveiled' truth of the New, the windows could be seen like veils both shrouding and revealing the ineffable. *The world was a veil illumined by the divine light.* We would therefore expect to find the windows used in this way—a veil of light forming the house of the Sun and the city of God, brilliant with the splendour of truth and the Godhead, and brought into being—in the phrase of Grosseteste's about colour—by 'light incorporated with the transparent medium'.

This type of symbolism is of course precisely what we can observe in Chartres. And not only there. It is something made into an almost textbook reality by the introduction in the second half of the thirteenth century of the *grisaille* window, a conscious attempt at harmony and diffusion (as Violet-le-Duc has described it) and virtually a literal veil of light forming the walls of the church. This was surely the architectural function of the Five Sisters Window in York Minster.

There has recently been published a valuable technical analysis of the glass of Chartres by James Rosser Johnson. Dr. Johnson is concerned with the experience of seeing the windows, and he gives a scientific explanation of the phenomena of vision and perception experienced by the observer, related to the physical characteristics of the light in the cathedral. In the terms of that study it is possible to explain technically the characteristics of the light in Chartres and the means by which an experience shared by many people of different ages has been made possible.

Light has certain properties which it is necessary to control. These are primarily the level of illumination, the incidence of glare, the phenomenon of surface light and the perception of colour. Stained glass however has this special property: that it creates the optical conditions for its own perception as well as for the perception of everything else in the building; and in this it is at once very difficult and very satisfying to the mind. It contains the possibility of being the illuminated veil; but that potential can only be realised if the problems given are satisfactorily solved. They were.

First, the artists clearly realised—what we have frequently failed to realise—that to be physically effective the scheme must be complete. Our habit of providing clear areas of glass to increase the level of illumination inside a church was not accepted at that time. For the conditions for the best possible perception of the glass are that the interior should be relatively dark, and that no unwanted light should be present inside to shine on the internal surface of the stained glass windows. Over fifty years ago, Lewis Day rightly observed that 'every ray of light which penetrates into a building excepting through the stained glass does injury to the coloured window'.[1] What it does is to produce a *surface light*, which partly destroys the radiance of the glass. This will of course happen anyway even in the completely glazed church, with the movement of the sun; at different times of the day, windows will let in more light and tend to cast a surface light on windows opposite. That is why visitors who have spent the minimum of tourist time in a place such as Chartres, will sometimes give a disparaging account of the dullness of windows one had always thought to be brilliant; one must see them over a period, with allowance for their difference of brightness and reflectance at different times of the day. But above all, completeness of the scheme is the first requirement; and there can be little doubt that such was what the mediaeval designers recognised.

Secondly it is necessary to counteract the effects of glare. 'Glare is caused by a disproportionate mixture of high and low luminosities in the same visual field which go beyond the normal adaptive powers of the eye'.[2] It arises when some parts of the field of view are bright in relation to the general level; it can cause loss of acuity of vision or merely discomfort. With stained glass it occurs when an area of white or near-white glass is incorporated into a window of a generally lower level of illumination; and it happens because in such conditions the eye is unable to adapt itself to the range of contrast presented to it.

Central to this fact is the phenomenon of adaptation, which in optics means the ability of the eye to alter its sensitivity according to the conditions of its environment. Adaptation alters both its sensitivity to amounts of light and its sensitivity to change or contrast. Now the eye can adapt itself to a very wide

[1] Lewis Day, *Windows*, London 1909, p. 372.
[2] J. R. Johnson, *The Radiance of Chartres*, Columbia University Studies in Art and Archaeology IV, Phaidon 1964, p. 12.

range of brightness; for instance, it can adapt itself within a range of such as that for daylight (anything from 500 to 10,000 lumens/sq. ft.) or that of Chartres (measured by Johnson as having an average of 1 to 2 lumens).[1] But while it can therefore appreciate a range of well over 1000 to 1 it cannot do this at the same time; furthermore, the range of brightness which it can comfortably accept decreases with the general level of illumination. Outside we may be able to appreciate a range of 100 to 1; inside, for normal tasks like reading, the range of brightness may need to be no more than from 30 to 70 lumens. And at the lower level, sensitivity to contrast—the ability to appreciate without pain differences of brightness—will be still further reduced.

With stained glass it is not only the simplest thing in the world to cause glare; it is also easy to create discomfort if the range of brightnesses in the window is too great. For example, as Johnson points out, clear glass will transmit 80–90 per cent of the light, opalescent glass 55–85 per cent, and deep blues and reds 5–10 per cent or less. If the sun behind it has a brightness (say) of 4,000 lumens, it can be appreciated that the range of contrast is huge and potentially destructive.

If we now think again of what the mediaeval architect and glass-worker were trying to achieve, we can see that in our terms there had to be a high degree of selectivity and a very careful control of the range of brightness. This is of course the complicated explanation of the reason for 'hatching' or 'scumbling'—putting films of paint over clear areas of glass; without that explanation the need was made clear simply by experience and experiment. But it is also a reason for the selection of predominant colours.

The predominant colours of early mediaeval glass are of course red and blue. The general light transmission is low. And there is here an interesting phenomenon. The eye tends to perceive the central colours of the spectrum (the green–yellow area) when it is adapted to light, and the outer (blue–violet area) when it is adapted to dark.[2] This means that blues for example appear to be *relatively* brighter when the eye is adapted to conditions of dark, such as those in a cathedral. At the same time, in such conditions acuity is lessened and there is some vagueness in the perception of contrast and therefore of form. There is however an intermediate range of sensitivity, which Johnson believes is the condition in Chartres cathedral.

[1] Ibid. Lumens are expressed by Johnson as *Foot-candles*.   [2] Johnson, op. cit., p. 17.

What in fact happens? The process of adaptation to the full condition of maximum receptivity in Chartres takes about half an hour. Entering from bright daylight into the dark interior, the eye has to tune itself. The windows therefore change in form and in colour relations. The architecture of the interior is hardly visible at first (and some of the later over-fine carving, for example of the sixteenth-century screen, never becomes fully effective). Gradually it begins to define itself. And as it does so the full radiance of the windows becomes manifest. In short, there is here a 'kind of revelatory process', caused by partial dark-adaptation in the 'pervasive glow of warm colour'. And this process of revelation is capable of continuing, with the exploration of the building and the continual changes of light. It begins to effect a transformation of appearance.

And what, after adaptation, is the impression received? It is precisely a veil of light, which is the analogy we were seeking. For, in Johnson's words, 'old stained glass, because of the density and irregularity of the material, holds back or disperses most of the light acting upon it, resulting not only in low luminosities but in a vagueness of form for all objects perceived'. Not only the architecture. For 'this unusual light also affects the visitor who himself undergoes a kind of metamorphosis, for he does not cast a definable shadow in this mysterious and diffused glow, the optical laws governing daylight having been rearranged and held back'.[1]

Now this well-known characteristic of twelfth- and thirteenth-century glass—that it appears to hold the light back within itself rather than send its rays upon the interior—is a magical and evocative phenomenon. I think one can see in it a correspondence to what the scientists of the time believed of the physics of light and of optics—that rays were both intramitted and extramitted. Poised against the material rays coming from the sun, there are rays going out from the eye and fastening upon the glowing form of the windows.

In a brilliant analysis of *Byzantine Aesthetics*, Fr. Gervase Matthew suggested a few years ago that the belief in extramission of rays explained the peculiarities of perspective used in Byzantine wall painting and mosaics particularly from the late twelfth century. The lines of the perspective are so to speak converging inside the building, where the spectator is, rather than in a vanishing point outside the wall, as in Renaissance perspective. That is to say, depth was

[1] Johnson, op. cit., pp. 19–24.

conceived as being in front of the mosaic or a picture, not behind it, and the picture space was essentially that of the church, 'since art was considered a functional part of architecture'. It also means that the view point is *behind* the scene, and figures are shown smaller in proportion to their distance from the view point.[1] Such an idea is consistent with neo-Platonic theories of vision; but it would also be natural to a craftsman who believed as everyone else did about the facts of vision.

It is possible to see the same peculiarities in the perspective of some of the panels of the windows at Chartres. It would be consistent with the idea not only of the viewpoint being behind the window but also, as is certainly the case, with the light being behind it. And the light, like the viewpoint, is of course not only sunlight but the light of God, the divine illumination that gives form and splendour to the House of God. It tends to confirm the view of the light, embodied in and diffused through the picture, being held in a point of balance and across the plane which formed the field of vision.

Now the holding back of the light could be accidental. Time has deposited a patina on the back of old glass which has a lot to do with this optical effect. It is pitted and scarred by exposure to the weather and sometimes to chemical action, and this causes a complicated refraction of the light rays, which in turn causes the diffusion which is observed. But here Johnson maintains—and I do not remember seeing it stated so uncompromisingly before—that this patina is not the real cause of the diffusion, but that 'the inner structure of old glass is dense and complicated, broken up by impurities, bubbles, streaks, and unequal colour distribution, rendering the glass a deeply translucent medium' rather than a transparent one.[2] And this is not merely accidental or forced upon the makers, because clear and transparent glass could be produced in the Middle Ages. He thinks therefore that 'conscious efforts were made by the glass-maker to enrich his medium before surface coatings were applied.'

Evidence for this he finds in the well-known development of ruby glass— the white glass 'flashed' with red because, it has always been said, a full red glass made at the time would have been too dense to transmit any serious light and colour at all. Johnson does not accept this, but maintains that it was possible to diffuse red pigment throughout the entire thickness of the piece of glass and

[1] Gervase Matthew, *Byzantine Aesthetics*, London 1963, pp. 25–34.
[2] Johnson, op. cit., p. 53.

still produce glass of the necessary brightness. The reason why the glass was flashed had to do with the brightness but more particularly with the required *radiance* of red. Microscopically old ruby shows itself as a very complicated and irregular medium, quite unlike our neat 'flash' of red cleanly spread over white; such glass can be found not only in Chartres but in many other places, with a great variety of stratification patterns. He discusses the methods by which this may have been done. But 'whatever the procedure, the mediaeval artist succeeded in creating a complex structure which allowed only a fraction of incident light to penetrate his medium, a medium that scattered the rays again and again in a complicated implosion producing the variety and richness normally associated with old glass, giving it a quality of glowing from within'.[1]

That this quality was deliberate is suggested by the marked similarity of ideas about glass and the mediaeval attitude to jewellery. The two were regularly discussed together, and the similarity was inevitable; for the windows to inspire the vision they needed to glow like jewels with an inner light. Mediaeval jewels were usually fashioned *en cabochon*, rather than facetted (which was a Renaissance habit) and this gives an impression of light glowing from within, which was what some mediaevals believed to happen. Jewels formed part of the whole panoply of colour and light in the splendour of the sanctuary, with its vestments and sacred vessels; they were another item in the vision. They had the kind of luminosity which was a favourite analogy in the light metaphysic. And so in the same way, and with careful intent, the 'ancient windows diffuse and transform the light of day into the "new light" of the Celestial Jerusalem'.[2]

[1] Johnson, op. cit., pp. 56–7.   [2] Ibid., p. 63.

4 Calculated Nature

If there is one idea, or one aspiration, which characterises the intellectual world of the Renaissance, it is the search for *unity*. It informed much thinking, it dominated whole areas of the field of politics, it gave direction to the invisible lines of pictorial composition, it was a regular obsession with the designers of buildings and gardens and towns.

It was, after all, the age of the great, centralised, absolute monarchies. But it was also an age of fragmentation: of the break up of the apparent unity of Christendom, of the Reformation and Counter-Reformation, of religious wars that gradually revealed themselves as essentially political wars and turned Europe into barricaded areas of nationalistic pride.

In some respects therefore there was nothing simple or unified about the Europe of the Renaissance. Yet the search for some kind of unity was central to the Renaissance mind. It was a time of such diverse individual discoveries that it is not surprising to find people anxious to deduce something unified behind it; we are to some extent engaged in the same search today. The people making this search during the Renaissance were the real critics of society—the artists and the architects, fashioning images and creating an environment that would make sense of it all.

The Renaissance aspiration was not a new one altogether; it was simply another way of approaching the possibility of an organised and coherent landscape. In this it was very different from the mediaeval one. The Renaissance has been described as fundamentally a revolt against scholasticism. It broke down the patterns of thinking discussed in the last chapter, and substituted for a serial method of organising information and argument a more centralised and formal one.

This chapter is concerned with the world created during some 350 years—from approximately the middle of the fifteenth century to the end of the eighteenth. It looks at the development of ideas, then at the shape of the environment of major buildings, and lastly at the huge changes in the landscape as a whole.

The first architectural treatise of the Renaissance appeared about 1450 with the publication of the famous ten books by Alberti—*De Re Aedificatoria*. Alberti was in many respects the ideal Renaissance man. He was noted for his learning, for his familiarity with a whole range of subjects other than his own; he was adept at several of the arts and he was a connoisseur; he practised a conscious literary style; above all he was an architect of outstanding ability and —a feature not always characteristic of architects—of marked intellectual power. He was, in short, not far from being the universal man, and what he had to say about the design of buildings was calculated to affect large areas of the environment as a whole.

What is particularly relevant here is his interest in mathematics and his mathematical definition of beauty. 'Beauty', he wrote, 'consists in a rational integration of the proportions of all parts of a building, in such a way that every part has its absolutely fixed size and shape, and nothing could be added or taken away without destroying the harmony of the whole.'[1] If this seems at first a very limited concept, it was not so to its author. It was a reflection of a greater relationship between all things.

To him, a designer of great churches, it was possible to see in a church, the most perfectable of all buildings, the revelation of Divinity itself. It was possible to aim, through the media of its construction, at a solid representation of the great, infinite unity that was Godhead. To achieve this it was necessary to investigate first the shape of an ideal church; and since the most perfect and complete figure in geometry was the circle, the circle became the theme of his and his followers' continual experiments in elucidating architectural form. Secondly, it was necessary to relate all the details within that shape to each other. Alberti maintained that all the parts should be harmonically related, like the members of a human body.

In saying this Alberti was echoing the thought of the immensely influential Vitruvius, the first-century Roman architect and writer, whose text was known

[1] Alberti, *De Re Aedificatoria*, Bk. 6, Chapter 2.

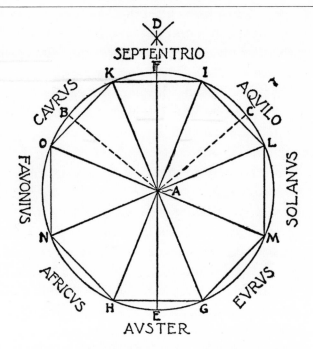

Vitruvius: diagram leading to a city plan (see p. 65)

and admired and was published (in Latin) in 1486. It was suddenly a bible for architects.[1] It was repeatedly republished in different languages, two of the most important editions being that of 1521, with an extensive commentary by Cesariano, a pupil of Bramante, and that of 1556 by Barbaro. It spread across Europe very rapidly; for example, there was a copy of the earliest edition in the library of the Blackfriars at Glasgow about the turn of the century.

What the Renaissance designers fastened on above all was a simple reference in Vitruvius' Third Book—on Temples—in which he suggested that buildings should reflect the proportions of a human figure. This was not all. It was shown that the figure of a well-built man with extended hands and feet could be fitted into the perfect geometric figures—the circle and the square. Vitruvian man began to decorate the pages of artistic thought. Cesariano drew him in the 1521 edition; Leonardo drew him, giving him, in a rather totalitarian way, four arms and four feet.

[1] Vitruvius, *The Ten Books of Architecture*, trans. M. H. Morgan, Cambridge, Mass., 1914.

It is, as Sir Kenneth Clark has pointed out, 'impossible to exaggerate what this simple-looking proposition meant to the men of the Renaissance. To them it was far more than a convenient rule: it was the foundation of a whole philosophy.'[1] They went further. They picked up the discovery of Pythagoras, that there was a mathematical parallel between proportional ratios in space and those of musical tones (the length of a string being exactly proportional to a musical tone), and thought that this immense discovery gave a clue to the harmony of the universe.

Here indeed was something magnetic to the Renaissance mind. The idea was taken up by subsequent writers. It was used by Serlio whose books from 1537 onwards were widely used in England. It appears again in Palladio, whose *Four Books on Architecture* was published in 1570.

Palladio was, if anything, even more of a universal man than Alberti; he was given his name, in fact, because the mentor who coined it saw in him the image of Pallas. He pursued the musical analogy and the theme of the Vitruvian man; he gave a definition of beauty that was close to Alberti's—'Beauty will result from the beautiful form and from the correspondence of the whole to the parts, of the parts among themselves, and of these again to the whole; so that the structures may appear an entire and compleat body, wherein each member agrees with the other and all members are necessary for the accomplishment of the building'.[2] He thought that the square and the circle were the most beautiful forms and that from them all others 'receive their measure'. He believed therefore in absolute symmetry; his Villa Rotonda near Vicenza (see p. 73) was wholly symmetrical (i.e. symmetrical from all four sides) and was a realisation of the geometrical skeleton and of musical ratios. Finally, in looking for examples of perfection to act as models for design, he knew where to find them. He found them in the buildings of antiquity, especially in the classical buildings of ancient Rome, and published his researches in the *Antiquities of Rome* in 1554. Buildings like the Parthenon revealed on examination the essential mathematical proportions. The case was made.

The influence of these theoretical ideas was enormous and they reappear again and again. But more than that; we have in them almost all the ingredients

[1] K. Clark, *The Nude*, London 1956, p. 13.
[2] A. Palladio, *The Architecture of Andrea Palladio*, in four books, revised, designed and published by Giacomo Leoni, London 1715.

22. Rome: the Capitol (p. 67)

A. F. Kerstin

24. Mereworth Castle, Kent (p. 71)

25. Castle Howard, Yorkshire (p. 72)

23. Rome: the Spanish Steps (p. 67)

26. Ha-ha: (a) Middlethorpe Hall, York

(b) Seaton Delaval, Northumberland (pp. 72–73)

Keith Gibson

27. Rievaulx Abbey, Yorkshire (p. 74)

28.
Alnwick, Northum-
berland: a Capa-
bility Brown
landscape
(pp. 75–76)

A. F. Kersti

29. London: Mecklenburgh Square (p. 77)

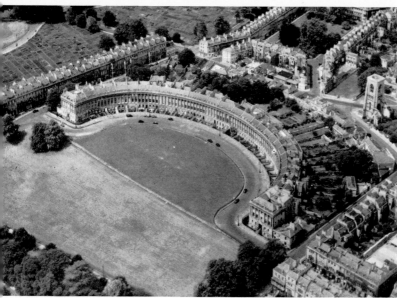

30.
Bath: Royal
Crescent (p. 78)

Aerofilms Ltd

Aerofilms Ltd

31. Edinburgh: the Moray Estate and New Town (pp. 78–79)

32. Keith, Banffshire; Reidhaven Square (pp. 79–80)

British Travel Association

33. Milton Abbas, Dorset (p. 80)

that make up the taste of the Renaissance as regards the environment, and we have them built into a coherent body of doctrine.

They are: the insistence on beauty of form, the belief that beauty consists in making a unity between the parts and the whole, the idea that the shapes of things must be as perfect as possible and that the simple geometric forms of the square and the circle are basic to that perfection, the belief that proportions can be mathematically established, the idea that the perfect proportions reflect those of the human figure, the discovery that the best examples can be found in the buildings of antiquity. And behind all these, justifying them, is the notion that perfection of form is a reflection of a metaphysical perfection, that the building is a microcosm reflecting the macrocosm, and that there can be a unity between the environment of man and the ultimate meaning of the world.

All this was, of course, essentially Platonic. Plato's thought, in which one deduces Forms or Ideas lurking behind the appearances of Things being the perfect forms to which natural and man-made objects are imperfect approximations, was in the ascendant in the fifteenth century. Alberti was a disciple; he thought that the soul of man reacts and conforms to the essential harmonic rule of creation.

And there was something else. You could not only have such thoughts; you could realise them in practice. The discovery (from about 1400) of the laws of perspective made it possible to produce a scientific interpretation of space. So architecture almost became a science. The environment could be rationally contrived; it could be calculated and controlled; it was subject to reason. But in case you should be alarmed at too much mathematics and geometry, you had the profound consolation that it all reflected the shape—and the nature—of man. The human being remained at the centre of the theory. It was, after all, the Age of Humanism.

You would therefore expect that in thinking about the layout of towns and cities and the landscape as a whole, Renaissance designers might produce patterns of unity like those for the buildings. They did. There was a series of studies for Ideal Cities.[1] There was one in Vitruvius, a plan developed from the direction of the winds into a centralised plan with eight sectors. It was adapted many times, but brought into line with contemporary needs to cater for the kind of fortifications made necessary by the invention of gunpowder. New kinds of

[1] H. Rosenau, *The Ideal City in its architectural evolution*, London 1959.

redoubt were planned by architects—Michelangelo was the designer of the fortifications of Florence in 1529; Alberti produced a plan for a fortress city. Filareti published (about 1460) a remarkable plan for the ideal city of Sforzinda, dedicated to the Sforzas. It was geometric, centralised, and fortified. It had a labyrinth outside, it made provision for all classes of society, it had a radiating system of streets and canals, a series of subsidiary squares, and an elaborate town centre with a main square. In it was to be placed a symbol of universality, a remarkable building called the 'House of Vice and Virtue', ten stories high, containing lecture rooms, a brothel at the bottom, and an academy of learning at the top—a proposal that may have been realised unconsciously by the designers of universities in modern times. Further rules were laid down by Scamozzi in 1615 in his *Idea of a Universal Architecture*; he not only adopted the geometric form, but also divided the city into functional zones.

In practice, a number of ideal cities was begun. Palma Nuova, the fortress city of Venice, was begun in 1593 as an attempt at ideal form. Later, about 1715, Karlsruhe was begun for the Margrave of Baden; the city itself was placed in a sector, the gardens completed the circular form. But the significant point is not the small number of whole towns actually built. It is that the concepts of the Renaissance architects, striving for ideal form, were applied to other places. The polygonal fortified shape, the sector, the radiating streets, the central square, the ordered, geometric patterns, were applied to the improvement and trans-formation of existing towns.

For instance, Rome itself. A major piece of replanning was carried out under Pope Sixtus V, one of those great Renaissance popes whose most lasting doctrines were architectural ones. Between 1585 and 1590 he established the lines of new streets and laid out new piazzas. One of the most interesting groups of the former are the streets that radiate from the Piazza del Populo, the centre one being the old Via Flaminia; they are a direct influence from formal idealised thinking.

In reorganising his city he was founding it on antiquity. The shapes and lines are those of the ancient Roman plan. In one case at least, that of the Piazza Navona, he made an open space by following the outline of the old Roman amphitheatre on that spot. Furthermore, he showed his understanding of one of the main problems of radial and formal planning—the problem of how to terminate vistas and how to mark nodal points. It was a problem that grew constantly in importance; Sixtus dealt with it by a lavish use of columns and obelisks. They became focal points (it was he who had the obelisk moved to the piazza of St. Peters, promising the engineer the gallows if anything failed in the move); they became terminal eye-catchers. He also organised the water supply for the city, and thus made possible the fountains that then and later became one of the principal fascinations of Rome and one of the elements of all grand designs.

But at this point there was introduced another element. An important development in Renaissance planning was from the strict formalism of ideal planning to the exploitation of *illusion* in creating environmental spaces. It was not really a change in aim; it was a better realisation of the means to achieve aesthetic ends. For one of the faults of the ideal cities was that they were conceived on paper and drawn on the flat. As soon as one entered the real world of three dimensions, a new set of architectural problems and possibilities was presented.

Skilful in perspective, it was therefore natural for the architects of the High Renaissance and the Baroque to exploit illusion to obtain a dramatic effect. The connection between town planning and theatre design was already known; it had been vividly shown in the street settings with artificial perspective in Palladio's Teatro Olympico in Vicenza. The dramatic possibilities in civic grouping were put into effect. On the Capitoline Hill, Michelangelo reconstructed the buildings from 1538 onwards, deliberately taking advantage of converging lines on plan to provide a theatrical setting for the ancient statue of Marcus Aurelius which had been moved there. He also used the play of levels; he constructed steps and established their section so that the view on approach unfolded scenically. It was a notable improvement on the ideal plans.

By the end of the century, Sixtus V played with spaces similarly. From one of his radiating roads he envisaged a link to the high level Piazza of Trinita del Monte. This was built later (in the eighteenth century) as the famous Spanish Steps, a lasting demonstration of the fluidity of form and the scenic potentialities of manipulating levels. It is a studied exercise in the creation of movement, spaces and vistas. When Bernini was commissioned to complete the square in front of St. Peter's in the seventeenth century he employed converging lines for optical reasons and built the great curved colonnades which are an exercise in perspective in movement and a grand statement of Baroque power.

These two trends—the trend towards ideal geometric form and the trend towards dramatic illusion—can be studied at Versailles, the gargantuan palace of Louis XIV that grew out of his quest for quiet, peace and solitude. There are two immediate connections with Sixtus V. First, the planning of the palace and town of Versailles was a version of Sixtus' road plan at the Piazza del Populo. Here the three converging roads meet at the entrance to the palace in a great 'place'. Secondly, the planners of Versailles had learnt the lesson about the water supply. A huge machine—'Marly's Machine'—was built to draw water up to the level necessary for the town of Marly and for the palace and its fountains.

The significance of the water supply was as fundamental as the discovery of perspective. It entirely revolutionised the siting of buildings. For while, during earlier periods, important buildings had normally to be placed at low levels so as to have the advantage of natural water supply and drainage (the sites of mediaeval abbeys were always dictated by this requirement), an entirely new prospect was opened up to those who now had the control of water in their technical repertoire. It meant that they could site buildings on high ground, and they could do so for purely aesthetic reasons. They could 'command a noble prospect' and organise the views. Nothing had more effect on the country house layouts of the eighteenth century than this control over nature.

Versailles in the seventeenth century had all this and a lot more besides. The palace of the Sun King, it radiated out across nature, the landscape equivalent of an ideal city, reflecting the glory and the absolutism of that faintly ridiculous man. Its grounds were laid out by Le Nôtre on civic lines. But it was the most formal kind of city. Even though it was a landscape, it was as if the designer had put on paper a close mesh of evenly spaced dots. These were the trees. He then cleaned off long straight lines in a pattern of radiating avenues, and made a few squares and circles and polygons at their intersections. The plan was given to the gardeners, who moved and transplanted trees in unprecedented numbers.

Versailles set the pattern for this absolute domination of nature by art. The owners of chateaux followed suit, creating formality and artifice even where nature was wonderfully grand. Nature fought back sometimes, as at Chenonceaux; but even there the architect was dominant and coolly spanned the river with his otherwise gloomy house. At Versailles, however, nature merely laughed at the pretensions of a pompous king.

For there was a basic fallacy in this formal designing which finally caused its own collapse. It was the problem of how to finish it off at the edges, how to come to an end. For Louis there was theoretically no end. His great central avenue could only carry on round the world until it eventually came in again at the back door—a fitting comment on the futility of power. It would have been a suitable symbol for a man of his territorial ambitions. But since that cannot be done, there has to be an end of art and a beginning of nature somewhere. At Versailles it comes, after a long walk, at the end of the great avenue, when you drop with a wet flop into an untidy lake.

The fact is that everyone who creates a man-made environment has to find a way of fitting it into the natural world. As he looks over towards the horizon he has to find some way of relating, either by contrast or continuity, the environment of his own making to the bigger one that surrounds it. Renaissance designers on the Continent tried to create a totally organised environment which would fulfil Alberti's idea of beauty—'a rational integration of all the parts', so that all the parts belonged to, and could not be taken away from, the whole. To an extent they achieved it; they left us great formal conceptions of space, ideas of symmetry, balance and architectural unity, examples of an environment dominated by man. What they could not do was to organise the whole of nature. To see how that was undertaken, we must turn to Great Britain in the eighteenth century.

Great Britain was conveniently in the midst of an agricultural revolution that involved nothing less than the transformation of the countryside. Because of that and the emergence of a new pattern of country living, much of what we take for granted today as the natural landscape of England was in fact a deliberate creation by landowners in the eighteenth century. They made, as Trevelyan points out in his Social History,[1] a very beautiful land. They took the remains of the old open fields, the heaths and thickets, and, with changes in the techniques of agriculture, enclosed fields with hedges of bramble and hawthorn, with tall elms, with new plantations of oak and beech. They created the great parks, with deer among the big trees. Wordsworth's England, a balance of the work of nature and man, took shape in that century, and as it passed, the painters found in it a subject more fascinating than the earlier round of portraits and historical scenes. The landscape came to illustrate the specifically eighteenth-century attitude to the place of man in nature.

[1] G. M. Trevelyan, *English Social History*, London 1944, pp. 400–3.

Eighteenth-century thought was dominated by a preoccupation with nature, and since it was also the century in which were developed rules of taste, the influence of philosophical ideas on the actual forms of environmental design can be assumed. But the characteristically English attitude to nature was—and had been for some centuries—quite different from that of the continent. Even when gardens were formal and Bacon wrote his much-quoted description of the garden—a chilly piece of megalomaniac planning—there was another, more sensuous and lyrical tradition. It can be found in Shakespeare and in Spenser.

Art and nature could complement each other, and each, as in Spenser's Bower of Bliss, might beautify the work of the other while striving to undermine it. But a fanciful interpretation of the roles of Art and Nature required further study by the creator of a landscape. By the beginning of the eighteenth century his attitude to nature had become a special one. He was looking for the *rules* of nature.

'Nature and Nature's laws lay hid in night,
God said, let Newton be! And all was light.'

Pope's satirical couplet expresses an attitude. The discoveries of science revealed, not chaos, but order, law and design; so the natural world could be taken as an authority, and from nature could be deduced laws through the action of reason. Thus was produced peace, order, progress and proportion; and ultimately Nature revealed the Godhead.

It is easy to see in this a similarity to the ideas of the Italian Renaissance theorists discussed earlier. For nature is not just what is found around in terrifying, untamed abundance; Nature is what is congenial to an abstract man, Man as he ought to be; and he is the man of education and sensibility. He uses his reason to deduce law and order in nature, and then organises Nature properly. The poet does this through his insight. Nature offers a brazen world; the poet delivers a golden one. The architects and landscape designers have the more difficult task of actually transforming it.

Fortunately for them, they were employed by people who were socially and financially in a good position to do so. The great patrons of the period must have enjoyed a life of as near perfect felicity as could be imagined. And they could justify that felicity and their own superiority. For, with their superior education and experience, they were people of discrimination and taste. They could understand. In Shaftesbury's *Characteristiks of Men* (1711), which had a marked influence on the patronage of the Whig aristocracy, the position is clearly stated. Nature can be perfected; when perfect, it is a reproduction of the harmony and proportion in the greater world (the Platonic theory again); the exercise of virtue is to follow this ideal nature. But how do you decide what ideal nature is like? You do so by the operation of common sense, and the Free Play of Minds. This takes place, says Shaftesbury, 'between gentlemen and friends'—'the mere Vulgar of Mankind often stand in need of such a rectifying object as the gallows before their eyes'.[1]

Nothing could have been more satisfactory, to a gentleman and his friends. They had taste. They could deduce rules. And they might have created as rule-ridden a landscape as their French contemporaries. They had the opportunity and power.

Lord Burlington, for example, produced canons of taste for less educated and less travelled persons. He was responsible, from 1715, for the widespread adoption of Palladian rules in architecture. He studied Palladio's theories and buildings and published Palladio's *Four Books*. He accepted the rules for unity and symmetry and proportion, and called for slavish adaptations of Palladio's work. Colin Campbell's Mereworth Castle was a version of Palladio's Villa Capra. Burlington's own Assembly Rooms at York were a version of Palladio's suggestion for an Egyptian Hall. Aided by Kent, Burlington did some more Palladian work at Chiswick. Kent himself carried out an expert study at Holkham, carrying the principles of symmetry into all the details and units of which this entirely symmetrical composition was made up.

But it could not last. Kent was not really a Palladian or a Renaissance theorist. He was at heart a romantic, or perhaps just an Englishman. He was so English that he used to affect Italian mannerisms. In his landscape design, as in one of his last buildings—the Horse Guards at Whitehall—he became thoroughly English and whimsical again. He was ultimately one of those practical men in England who never entered the maze of theory because they had such an eye for natural possibilities.

Vanbrugh was a pupil of Wren. Wren was familiar with Renaissance theory and produced a plan for London, influenced by the Roman experiment, which was never carried out. He developed a grand piece of urban design at Greenwich.

[1] 3rd Earl of Shaftesbury, *Characteristicks of Men*, London, 5th ed., 1732, p. 127.

When Vanbrugh received his first commission—to build Castle Howard —he threw down on the hillside a similar piece of urban design, which is probably based on Wren's urban conceptions. But he went much further; he seized upon the scenic possibilities of this dramatic site, and laid out lawns, paths, woods, temples and fortifications on an entirely unsymmetrical non-axial principle, placing monuments to emphasise the natural eminences of the ground, not all of which are immediately obvious. At the end came Hawksmoor's heroic mausoleum. The impact was powerful. 'Nobody had informed me', wrote Horace Walpole, 'that I should at one view see a palace, a town, a fortified city, temples on high places, woods worthy of being each a metropolis of the Druids, the noblest lawn in the world fenced by half the horizon, and a mausoleum that would tempt one to be buried alive; in short, I have seen gigantic places before, but never a sublime one.'[1]

We have here not only the image of the classical fortified city but also two influential and lasting ideas—the notion of 'sublimity' expressed in the environment, and that of a lawn 'fenced by half the horizon'. If we turn to Vanbrugh's next commission, Blenheim Palace, we meet the landscape gardener, employed by Vanbrugh, to whom is accredited (by Walpole) an invention that made it possible to regard the horizon as your fence. This was Bridgeman, and his invention was the 'ha-ha', or sunken fence.

One can hardly over-emphasise what this meant. As we saw at Versailles, the destructive fault in axial, classical planning was the impossibility of ever ending the avenues, or merging them into the three-dimensional irregularity of nature. The ha-ha was the answer. Because the fence was hidden in an excavated ditch, you could not see it; but it kept the cows at bay and your rights were preserved. Your grounds seemed boundless. And all at once you could conceive of an entire landscape, private and public, in three dimensions and in movement. You might still have axes and avenues and fixed points, but you limited their scale. Progressively you abandoned them altogether. Instead you made *groups* of things, of natural things; you arranged them in planes. You aimed at unifying the whole view—and you did it here, not by trying to dragoon the immediate environment into formal ranks, but by trying to grasp the nature of the specific site. You captured 'the genius of the place' and intensified it. And thus, in a very subtle and restrained manner, by apparently giving in to nature, you were in

[1] H. Walpole, *Correspondence*, Yale edition, London 1961, Vol. 30, p. 257.

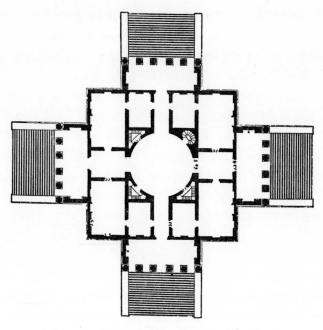

Villa Capra (Rotonda) Vicenza: plan (see p. 64)

fact monarch of all you surveyed. It was 'sweet concealment's magic art'.

Thus, when William Kent set about making magic landscapes at Stowe, Holkham and elsewhere, he seemed to be revelling in nature. His approach is best explained again by Horace Walpole. 'The sunk fence ascertained the specific design; and when nature was taken into the plan, under improvement, every step that was made pointed out new beauties and inspired new ideas. At that moment appeared Kent, painter enough to taste the charms of landscape, bold and opinionative enough to dare and to dictate, and born with genius to strike out a great system from the twilight of imperfect essays. *He leaped the fence and found all nature was a garden* . . . Thus the pencil of his imagination bestowed all the arts of landscape on the scenes he handled.'

Walpole summed Kent up thus: 'He was a painter, an architect and the father of modern gardening. In the first character he was below mediocrity; in the second, he was the restorer of the science; in the last, an original and the inventor of an art that *realises painting and improves nature*. Mahomet imagined an Elysium, but Kent created many.'[1]

Upon an art that 'realises painting and improves nature', the influence of painting became increasingly important. 'All gardening is landscape painting', said Pope, and thus expressed another unity in the Renaissance vision. Enthusiasts confirmed that their first observations of nature came through paintings; it was the origin of the *picturesque*.

Especially significant were the painters Claude Lorraine and Salvator Rosa. In the former's work nature had acquired form; in a calm and idyllic landscape, there were ruined temples and fragments of an antique world; there were the single trees that provided middle distance eye-catchers to help the illusion of distance. In the latter's was a romantic wildness with roaring torrents, rocks and cliffs and ruins and twisted trees and racing skies, an image of the lawless life legendarily lived by the painter himself. Landscape design was based on both. Kent even planted dead trees to look like Rosa's work ('who but a student of painting . . . would have thought of planting dead trees in a living landscape?' wrote one critic). Many others besides him were attracted to ruins; for here also was evidence of the ravages of time. They showed the ultimate dominance of nature over man, even though man had cunningly to contrive it.

At few places can this be better enjoyed than at Fountains Abbey. There William Aislabie, the owner of Studley Park, laid out the geometric lakes and canals of a moonlight garden, fashioned rustic bridges and classical temples. It was basically a formal conception. But then he also leaped the fence. Taking over the ruins of Fountains Abbey, 'with arrogant self-confidence and stupend-ous success' (to quote Pevsner)[2] he incorporated the whole thing as a genuine ruin in a calculated eighteenth-century landscape. There were walks, shrub-beries, bold and sharp cliffs, if rather small. He arranged a path to a 'Surprise View', from which, through an opening in the trees, the Abbey looks small and mysterious and suitably refined. At Rievaulx the owner of Duncombe Park played a similar game by making the Rievaulx Terraces at high level, above the abbey ruins; on the slopes a series of cuttings was made through the trees like the spokes of a wheel, so that you can look down from different angles at the monastic buildings in the centre.

[1] I. W. U. Chase, *Horace Walpole; Gardenist*, Princeton, N.J. 1943, pp. 25–6, 62.
[2] N. Pevsner, *Yorkshire; the West Riding*, London 1959, p. 203.

Nature was being systematically exploited. But it was exploited with subtlety. William Shenstone, the owner of a small farm called 'The Leasowes', spent a life-time transforming it into an ornamental farm and showing it to the literary personalities of his time. There was a winding path that linked a variety of natural scenes. But he was too short of money to build temples; he therefore made do with garden seats and urns and inscriptions so that people could look and read and indulge 'a thousand agreeable ideas'. It was all carried out with cunning and self-effacement. 'Art', he said, 'should never be allowed to set foot in the province of nature otherwise than clandestinely and by night.'[1]

The man who carried to the limit the capturing of nature was Lancelot Brown (1715–1783) who received his nickname 'Capability' from his constant references to the capabilities of any site. His practice was enormous; there is no record of the number of parks he improved; he effectively changed the environment of the island. He is said to have refused an invitation to Ireland on the plea that he had not yet finished England, and someone once remarked that he hoped he would die before Capability, as he would like to see Heaven before Capability improved it. He was practical and shrewd. He took what he found and made it look more natural than it had done before. When he dammed the river Glyme at Blenheim to form the lake, he remarked, 'The Thames will never forgive me for this.' He was, as Walpole said, 'Lady Nature's second husband'.

It is interesting that Brown began his career in 1751, in the same decade as Hogarth published his *Analysis of Beauty*, Burke his *Enquiry into the Origin of the Sublime and the Beautiful*, and Hume his *Essay on Taste*. Burke rejected the rational theories earlier discussed. Proportion and geometry, he considered, had nothing to do with beauty, which was apprehended intuitively and immediately. Hogarth explained the significance of an undulating line of beauty. Hume considered that aesthetic judgements were subjective. It all added up to a much freer, more intuitive attitude to artistic design, and it may be more than a coincidence that Capability Brown was so widely employed in realising it.

His sales technique was suitably literary in manner. 'He illustrates everything he says about gardening', says a contemporary account, 'with some literary or grammatical allusion. He told me he compared his art to literary composition. Now there, said he, pointing his finger, I make a comma, and there, pointing to another part (where an interruption is desirable to break the

[1] H. F. Clark, *The English Landscape Gardens*, London 1948, p. 17.

view), a parenthesis—now a full stop, and then begin another subject.'[1]

Brown thought that 'no disgusting display of art should be visible'. His elements were the encircling belt of woodland, with a boundary ride, and an irregular inner edge: within this, clumps of individual trees in free standing groups with long shadows: in the middle distance a lot of water, either a river or lake, with naked river banks: lawns sweeping right up to the house. His practical knowledge enabled him to leave the landscape so that one hardly knows he was there. It was natural in the sense that he designed it so that time would complete the work. All you had to do was leave it alone. The grass would be green and cattle would graze on it, the trees would grow, the river banks would look after themselves, and the water would flow gently.

In the midst of this unaggressive display of the smoothness and appropriateness of studied nature, you could be happy. It has been pointed out that his landscapes seem designed to accommodate Dr. Johnson's description of happiness—'being swiftly drawn in a chaise over undulating turf in the company of a beautiful and witty woman'.

Here then in the eighteenth-century landscape is an entirely coherent attitude to environment. Though its emphasis changes, it is always trying to achieve the same end—to create a recognisable unity, to make a world in which man is master but in which he feels in his natural home; and for those who were privileged it went a long way toward success.

It is not the end of the story. There were important developments at the end of the century and the beginning of the next one. But the simplicity of theme and the unity of ideas were lost. So were some of the privileges; and natural man took on a new aspect. Wordsworth saw 'human nature seeming born again' in the French Revolution. The environment changed also. The Industrial Revolution was under way; forces quite outside the intellectual's control savaged the environment carefully built up in a strangely self-conscious and coherent century.

'The conflict and torment of the religious struggles', wrote Lytton Strachey, 'into which the whole energies of the Renaissance had been plunged, were over; the infinite agitation ushered in by the French Revolution had not yet begun. The interval was one of toleration and repose; of toleration which

[1] C. Hussey, *The Picturesque*, London 1927, pp. 137–8.

would have seemed incredible to the age which preceded it; of repose which seems no less incredible to ours.'[1]

That there are parallels between landscape and town design was true of Ancient Greece; it was equally true now. Urban developments in England and Scotland during the seventeenth and eighteenth centuries were influenced in principle by Renaissance ideals of formality, order, symmetry and proportion. Wren, as we saw, produced a plan for the rebuilding of London after the Great Fire that incorporated the details and techniques of Renaissance planning. But generally town design in Great Britain was more empirical and conservative than on the continent, and the grand visions of planners were rarely realised. Instead the eighteenth century left the towns some features as organic and apparently accidental as the 'natural' park land of the countryside. These were smallness of scale, quiet dignity and order, restraint, subtle variety and the expression of local character. And this was so even in the larger pieces of deliberate planning.

London, for example, grew mainly through private speculation in a series of individual estates. The main components were: the square, which was used constantly in urban design once it had been established as a model for college architecture at New College Oxford in 1379; the regular street, with more or less repetitive houses; and the house itself. The house derived its proportions, as Sir John Summerson has shown, from the elements of a classical column.[2] A house façade was essentially a classical order raised on a podium; the ground floor was the podium, the upper floors the length of the column, the attic was the entablature. In short, this was essentially a Palladian formula; and like Palladian villas, the houses had their most important rooms on the first floor. A Renaissance motif thus inspired the typical Georgian town house. But it also had a functional pattern—narrow frontage and deep rooms, with basements beneath the house and cellars beneath the artificial level of the pavements.

This was all very orderly, but there was a deeper order underlying it. The fully developed estate catered for all classes of society. The scale and emphasis of the houses in each part were affected by registration. The Building Act of 1774, known later as the 'Black Act', laid down categories of building known as 'Rates'. A 'Rate' was defined in terms of value and area (a 'square' being 100

---

[1] Lytton Strachey, *Characters and Commentaries*, London 1933, p. 12.
[2] J. Summerson, *Georgian London*, 1945, p. 19.

square feet). Thus a First Rate house had a value greater than £850 and an area greater than 9 squares; a Fourth Rate house had a value less than £150 and an area less than $3\frac{1}{2}$ squares. Each type had its own code; and because standards were set for speculative building for each type, standardisation of design was confirmed. It could lead to a certain monotony; it undoubtedly contributed to the order and dignity of the towns and guaranteed a visual and social order.

The standardisation of the environment was carried through much of Great Britain by the spread of ideas to the provincial towns and cities. The principal differences were in materials and scale; other differences were caused by the taste of individual designers.

At Bath, repetitive houses were built by John Wood the Elder, who composed the sides of his urban squares into unified elevations. But he also had a central idea. In 1741 he published a book, *The Origin of Building*, in which he emphasised the importance of Greek and Roman prototypes in design. Turning his energies on Bath itself, even though the ancient baths had not been found in his time, he conceived its future form as a rediscovered ancient Roman town. For this he needed a Forum, a Circus and an Imperial Gymnasium. South Parade was the relic of his Forum, and the Circus was his circus, where he hoped to see exhibitions of sports. It was, to give it further authority, based upon the Colosseum, turned inside out. The Colosseum however is not circular but elliptical in plan. So, when his son, John Wood the Younger, took over the layout of the Royal Crescent, he studied the true curvature of the Colosseum and built in effect an inverted demi-Colosseum of considerable monumentality. It has many subtleties of design, but essentially it reveals not only the formalism and need for the authority of antiquity, but also the English habit of exploiting the possibilities of an exciting landscape for its own sake. Its influence was widespread, and Colosseum-crescents were designed in increasing numbers. In Edinburgh, for example, in the middle of the eighteenth century, some squares were built as extensions to the Old Town. But in 1763 the foundation stone was laid on an entirely New Town. It was rectilinear in plan and the heights of its houses were controlled; built almost wholly out of one quarry at Craigleith, it has therefore a marked unity and dignity. The best preserved houses are in the later phases of the New Town, where again under different architects the style of decoration, the levels of eaves lines and string courses, the spacing of windows no matter what rooms were placed inside, were established in the conditions of lease. The layout of the Moray Estate shows the influence of Bath; it has a plan based upon linking a crescent, an oval and a polygon. And here, as in the whole New Town, there is a feature reminiscent of Greek planning. An ordered, intellectual plan is laid over the contours as though they were not there. It seems to be characteristic of the neoclassical mind to arrange a contrast between the organised plan and the demands of the site. As in the landscapes, Nature wins, and the resolution of the conflict creates some of the most stupendous views and cliffs of masonry to be seen anywhere.

To complete the picture it is necessary to return to the countryside again. The reorganisation of the environment, explained in terms of landscape and urban visions, was carried into effect on a larger scale in most of the rural areas. Two factors at least combined to make it an attractive proposition: first, the landowners had an idea about landscape and in many cases rebuilt villages on their estates as part of the improvement of the visual amenities; secondly, they were in the midst of an agricultural revolution and the start of the Industrial Revolution.

The North East Lowlands of Scotland reveal very clearly what happened.[1] There the agricultural revolution came comparatively late. In the early eighteenth century fields were enclosed, new crops and breeds of cattle were introduced, tree planting took place on a huge scale. The old communal farmtowns were erased, and instead of eight to twenty joint tenants farming strips of land in the midst of undrained marshes, large single farms were built. Roads were straightened out, new bridges were erected, mill ponds were formed and wide areas of land were reclaimed.

This work transformed the countryside and produced the landscape that is there today. But what happened to the many joint tenants who were displaced from the old farmtowns? They were rehoused in a number of entirely new villages, founded partly as agricultural settlements for the housing of labourers and partly for the fostering of rural industries. A villager could therefore be a hired farmworker or a smallholder or a tradesman with the minimum of land.

These new villages were laid out by the surveyors of the big landowners and they often had a standard form. It was eminently practical. Sir John Sinclair, the leading protagonist of estate improvements, published in the early

---

[1] P. J. Nuttgens, *The Architecture and Planning of the Settlements of the North East Lowlands of Scotland*, 1959. Unpublished thesis; copy in Edinburgh University Library.

nineteenth century his recommendations for villages. They were necessary, he considered, to combat the evils of scattered population and of the towns. Villagers could be contented and unambitious, and have the pleasures of society, that excited social affections and introduced urbanity among them. The villages fostered trade and gave the opportunity of a liberal education without infection from the bad company of towns. There was room for all sorts of trade; the villages could even (though this does not seem a great advantage) provide centres of recruitment for the army and navy. He also thought that they should be laid out to a regular plan, with houses to the front and service buildings to the back.

Most of the planned villages have similar layouts, rectilinear and regular; good examples are those at Fochabers, Tomintoul and Keith. But the movement was not confined to them. It spread to most parts of the Lowlands. What was created in effect was a village system in Scotland.

England was already a land of villages, but there too agricultural improvements were initiated. A number of new settlements was established. But even where an existing village retained its traditional plan, there was a major rebuilding of the houses; many English villages today have a character basically dependent upon short rows of neat, practical and standard houses—the legacy of the eighteenth century.

There was never again such a consistent attitude to design, nor perhaps such an output of man-made surroundings accepted as generally admirable. It could only happen under the control of powerful agencies, but also because there was an accepted idea of the desirable form of an environment as a whole. It was an idea of unity and the value of formal design; it was altered and refined in terms of the relation of man and nature and revealed by the organisation of landscape; and finally it was carried into the design of towns and of villages and into the practical working landscape of the common man.

What followed was a transformation of certain areas even more complete. The clarity of the eighteenth-century town was brought to an end. The orderly categories of building were swamped by the forms of industry. The landscape altered under a social revolution. To meet its challenge, there were new attempts to create a satisfactory environment; these are the subject of the next chapter.

5 The Common or Garden City

This chapter introduces the modern city. So far three basic ideas have been discussed as being expressive of the landscape of urbanism. That landscape was seen first as indicative of holiness: second as the image of Heaven or the celestial city: third as a search for unity between Nature and Man.

It seems reasonable to interpret the modern city similarly in terms of ideas. The modern city, however, has to be considered in at least two stages. This chapter deals with the industrial city and its reorganisation as the environment for a social conscience. The next and last chapter sees it as the environment of pragmatism. The first is concerned therefore with the nineteenth century and the early part of the twentieth century; the next with the city as it is today.

That the two stages should be considered together is logical. For it was only in the nineteenth and twentieth centuries that towns and cities began to grow to their present size and take over their present percentage of the population. In 1801 in Great Britain less than one person in ten lived in a town with more than 100,000 people. The proportion doubled in forty years, and doubled again in the next sixty years. By 1901 England was in effect an urban society and three-quarters of its population could be described as urban. The bigger the city was already, the faster was the growth that occurred. If you add the smaller towns (say those of 10,000 people) to the sum, then nine people out of ten live today in a town of some kind.

That hectic and unprecedented expansion was the result of the agricultural and industrial revolutions. They made fortunes for some, misery for many, and provoked protests from the more articulate.

The transformation of the environment is vividly described by Ruskin:

'. . . beauty has been in the world since the world was made and human language can make a shift, somehow, to give account of it, whereas the peculiar forces of devastation induced by modern city life have only entered the world lately; and no existing terms of language known to me are enough to describe the forms of filth, and modes of ruin, that varied themselves along the course of Croxted Lane. The fields on each side of it are now mostly dug up for building, or cut through into gaunt corners and nooks of blind ground by the wild crossings and concurrences of three railroads. Half a dozen handfuls of new cottages, with Doric doors, are dropped about here and there among the gashed ground: the land itself, now entirely grassless, is a deep-rutted, heavy-hillocked cart-road, diverging gatelessly into various brickfields or pieces of waste; and bordered on each side by heaps of—Hades only knows what!—mixed dust of every unclean thing that can crumble in drought and mildew of every unclean thing that can rot or rust in damp: ashes and rags, beer-bottles and old shoes, battered pans, smashed crockery, shreds of nameless clothes, door-sweepings, floor-sweepings, kitchen garbage, back-garden sewage, old iron, rotten timber, jagged with out-torn nails, cigar-ends, pipe-bowls, cinders, bones, and ordure indescribable; and variously kneaded into, or sticking to, or fluttering foully here and there over all these, remnants broadcast of every manner of newspaper, advertisement or big-lettered bill, festering and flaunting out their last publicity in the pits of stinking dust and mortal slime.'[1]

His outburst reveals not only the near-hysteria and hatred of filth which is characteristic of Ruskin; it also lists the paraphernalia of industrial development —the railroads and brickfields, the building plots and new houses, the refuse, the newspapers and advertisements. And beneath it lies a more serious social protest: one that was shared by many other commentators of the time. It included such factors as a hatred of the mammoth industrial city and its debris: a fear of the techniques of manufacturing industry and of what damage they would do to the dignity of man: a prophecy of the depersonalisation of the worker because of mass production techniques. The implication is that aesthetic, moral and social judgements are all related to one another; and the environment is an expression of them—an expression of life and culture.

'The idea of style', wrote Sir Kenneth Clark, 'as something organically

[1] John Ruskin, *Fair and Foul*, June 1880, quoted in Michael Goodwin, *Nineteenth Century Opinion*, London 1951, pp. 165–6.

connected with society, something which springs inevitably from a way of life, does not occur, as far as I know, in the eighteenth century.'[1] It certainly occurs with increasing force from the 1830s, and rises to a crescendo in the work of Ruskin and William Morris. But there is more to it than that; it may be that this idea of style as expressing the basic character of society is central to the new, emerging character of English architecture and urban planning—and a key to its motivation.

The sequence of developments appears to me as follows: first, protests, criticisms and ideas of the kind just described: second, some experimental philanthropic settlements: third, the development of policies leading to public health legislation: fourth, the Garden Cities and the Garden suburbs; finally, and nearer our own time, the New Towns inspired by the Reith Report of 1946. In that sense this chapter covers conveniently the period and movement from Ruskin to Reith.

No one was more acid in his criticism of the industrial city than Pugin, who published *Contrasts* in 1835 and *True Principles of Pointed or Christian Architecture* in 1841. Augustus Welby Northmore Pugin was a convert to Catholicism: a man with a burning enthusiasm for Gothic architecture and a pioneer of modern ideas of architectural functionalism and structural honesty. He designed churches mainly; he also designed capacious private houses for patrons such as the Earl of Shrewsbury and was the co-architect for the Houses of Parliament. But, as Raymond Williams has pointed out in *Culture and Society* (a book to which this chapter is much indebted), the most important element in his social thinking was his use of the art of the period to judge the quality of the society producing it.[2] He gave examples in *Contrasts*. The best known is the drawing of the Catholic town of 1440, contrasted with the same town in 1840; it is not only that the buildings are more solid and attractive in the former, but also that the people, the way they are being treated and the very type of building displayed are all selected to emphasise the degradation that had occurred in 400 years.

Thus, to him the arts—and especially the civic arts—were a reflection of society. To make any judgement about them involved a view of society itself. It was the view of a Catholic if one was Pugin, a Protestant if one was Ruskin,

[1] Kenneth Clark, *The Gothic Revival*, London 1928, 1962 edition, p. 123.
[2] Raymond Williams, *Culture and Society*, London 1958, p. 138.

a Socialist if one was William Morris. But in any case it was essential first to improve society and to improve men if one was to improve the environment. Ruskin stated that situation plainly, 'The great cry that rises from all our manufacturing cities, louder than their furnace blast, is all in very deed for this—that we manufacture everything there except men; we blanch cotton, and strengthen steel, and refine sugar, and shape pottery; but to brighten, to strengthen, to refine or to form a single living spirit, never enters into our estimate of advantages. And all the evil to which that cry is urging our myriads can be met only in one way: not by teaching or preaching, for to teach them is but to show them their misery, and to preach to them, if we do nothing more than preach, is to mock at it. It can be met only by a right understanding on the part of all classes, of what kinds of labour are good for men, raising them and making them happy.'[1]

Teaching and preaching, in the face of a social revolution, had indeed been irrelevant. The educational structure of the country was overwhelmed by the growth of the huge industrial city. The churches coped little better. The Church of England, essentially a rural organisation with parishes geared to a simple, predominantly agricultural society, failed for a long time to awaken to the realities of the modern city. The Catholics and the Nonconformists stepped in. Cardinal Manning's funeral in London was attended by the biggest turn-out of workers ever seen. The Nonconformists had even greater effect. They catered for the industrial poor; they built the chapels and the meeting houses which became powerful components in the social and visual scene. Of the total church attendance, Nonconformist attendances were striking. In Bradford, Leeds, Oldham, Wolverhampton and Sheffield, more than 50 per cent of the church attendances were at Nonconformist chapels; in Birmingham, Manchester, Salford and Newcastle it was only slightly less.[2]

Like Ruskin they recognised the need to create an ideology for people and to improve their lot. But there was a difference, in ideas if not always in style. If one was Ruskin, where would one find an example of social order, or an accepted hierarchy of activities, or an organic society worthy of emulation? One would find it in mediaeval society; and mediaeval society and mediaeval architecture therefore became the model for development.

[1] John Ruskin, *On the Nature of Gothic*, quoted in Williams, op. cit., pp. 146-7.
[2] Asa Briggs, *Victorian Cities*, London 1963, pp. 65, 66.

That, however, was only superficial style. The idea had implications more basic and far-reaching. If art and the environment were a reflection of society, then design—the making of the environment—must be a reflection of function or use. So Ruskin defined vital beauty: '. . . the appearance of felicitous fulfilment of function in living things, more especially of the joyful and right exertion of perfect life in man.'[1] Art and life were organically related and the quality of the environment was a criticism of the latter.

'The art . . . of any country is an exact exponent of its ethical life.'[2] Inevitably Ruskin disliked the city he saw growing about him; but he attacked not only its appearance; he attacked the *laissez-faire* society which lay at its heart. It was the essence of Victorian political economy. He hated it personally because it destroyed the order and beauty of which he recognised the need. It was that philosophy and that society that were creating the new Victorian cities—the cities of the railway and tramway age, the cities of steam and gas. They were the concomitants of industrial expansion and of sudden growth in the population. They were the phenomena of their time.

The most extraordinary was probably Middlesbrough, a prodigy—'an infant, but an infant Hercules', as one of the Councillors described it at the opening of its Town Hall.[3] In 1801 there were four houses and twenty-five inhabitants. In 1829 there were forty inhabitants. In 1831 there were 154; the expansion had begun. Ten years later, in 1841, there were 5,463; by 1861 there were 3,203 houses and 19,460 inhabitants; by the beginning of the twentieth century there were 91,302. The whole of this fantastic expansion was caused by private enterprise, by the economic individualism that characterised the Victorian economy. Industry was the top priority; environment and housing followed later.

The general condition of life in the industrial city demanded reform. In Manchester in 1842 the average age of death for professional people, the gentry and their families was 38; the average age of death for tradesmen and their families was 20; for mechanics, labourers and their families it was 17.[4] In

---

[1] John Ruskin, *Modern Painters*, quoted in Williams, op. cit., p. 141.

[2] John Ruskin, *Lectures on Art*, quoted in Williams, op. cit., p. 142.

[3] Asa Briggs, op. cit., Chapter 8, pp. 245–83.

[4] *Report on the Sanitary Conditions of the Labouring Population of Great Britain* 1842, quoted in Briggs, op. cit., p. 98.

Halifax in 1847 the average over all was 26. Anyone with a social conscience looking around him at the industrial city in the middle of the nineteenth century would have seen ill-health, and deduced from it the crime and immorality that obsessed commentators and made the city both repulsive and fascinating.

> 'From Hull, from Halifax, from Hell, 'tis thus,
> From all these three, good Lord, deliver us.'

The components of the *laissez-faire* Victorian city were the street, the factory, the canal, the railway station and the chapel. The street might be a random street or a regular one, or there might be hundreds of regular ones, but the problem for anyone hoping to improve that city was to take these components and put them together in an ordered and meaningful relationship.

The first major vision was by James Silk Buckingham, who published his proposals for an ideal city named Victoria in 1849. He wished to achieve '. . . order, symmetry, space and healthfulness'. This demanded the '. . . comfort and convenience of all classes';[1] he therefore proposed low densities of people per acre, the zoning of the town into functional areas, the planning of gardens, and a balance between social classes. Although Victoria was never built and no example that was built incorporated his ideas as such, his influence was enormous and it is possible to study actual projects which incorporated one or more of them.

Some of the earliest were in the north, especially in the wool and worsted manufacturing centres of the West Riding of Yorkshire. That, after all, was where many of the prodigy cities of the Industrial Revolution were at their most dense. Walter Creese, whose book *The Search for Environment*[2] has made a major contribution to studies of this period, has described some of the model settlements in the Halifax–Leeds–Bradford triangle. Their purpose was to create an environment in keeping with social ideals. The motives for building them were inevitably mixed. They involved both self-interest and benevolence; they were to improve the health of the residents and their well-being, but they were also to encourage a more efficient organisation, which in turn would ensure regularity of work. Whatever the mixture of motives, the developments reflected the social conscience of the great industrialist and entrepreneur. The

[1] Asa Briggs, op. cit., p. 71.
[2] Walter Creese, *The Search for Environment*, Yale 1966.

funeral oration for Sir Titus Salt, the builder of Saltaire, states the ideal clearly: 'He was a pioneer: a creator of the new era. He showed how the graces of the old feudalism that was being supplanted, could be grafted on and exemplified by the men who brought forth and moulded the better age. No feudal lord could have set open his doors and offered his resources to the retainers of generations, in the way he provided for those that laboured under his directions.'[1]

One of the first improvers was Colonel Edward Akroyd, the M.P. for Halifax. Personal experience had convinced him of the need for social improvements and better housing. Like most of his fellow industrialists he had made a fortune from power-driven machinery. He had witnessed strikes and violence in 1825 and 1826 against the weaving machinery being installed in the factories of Bradford; he had watched the Halifax disturbances of 1842, when the mob was only driven away from his mansion by musket fire.

His first model village was Copley, built between 1844 and 1853, on a site of twenty acres two miles south of the centre of Halifax. It was a mill estate between the railway embankment and the canal, and consisted of three long rows of houses with four shops, a village school, library and newsroom, allotments and space to keep pigs. One of the streets was named Pig Street; later, for the sake of respectability, it was renamed Railway Street. The design of the buildings was neo-Gothic throughout. Writing later under the title *On Improved Dwellings for the Working Classes*, he maintained that Gothic was a suitable style because it gave a picturesque outline in a modified old English style; it was in character with the old dwellings and with the site.[2] The houses were, like most of the workers' houses in Halifax, of the back-to-back type. But the whole village, widely spaced near the grandiose gates of a large plain factory and thus housing the operatives it required, was a notable improvement upon the rest of the town.

Copley was a very small-scale experiment. At Akroydon, built between 1861 and 1863, he introduced a scheme to promote home ownership. The Halifax Union Building Society had been founded in 1845. He now set up in 1860 the Akroydon Building Association, capitalised by the Halifax Permanent Benefit Building Society which had been founded in 1852. The Building

[1] Ibid., p. 13.
[2] Ibid., pp. 22–9.

Association supplied three-quarters of the cost of a house; the future owner was expected to produce a quarter of the cost. But when it was necessary Colonel Akroyd stepped in and frequently lent that quarter himself. It was convenient to all. Under the Parliamentary Reform Act of 1832 and the Municipal Corporations Act of 1835 a householder needed a forty-shilling freehold in order to have a vote. The Building Society could arrange the freehold and Colonel Akroyd could expect the vote.

Akroydon was an improvement upon Copley. It was also near the centre of Halifax on a hillside above the Hebble Valley. This time there were no back-to-back houses.[1] The architect was George Gilbert Scott and he built in domestic Gothic with dormers and gables. The two-storey houses were grouped in streets around a square. It provided a central park instead of private gardens and the houses were so arranged as to encourage a mixing of the social classes; houses were offered at four different price levels—£100, £140, £170 and £250. It is still worth a visit.

Akroyd was not alone in this work in Halifax. Another family, also industrialists, was the Crossleys. They built the West Hill Park Estate in 1863. They also turned their attention to the need for providing entertainment and open space. In 1857 they employed Paxton to lay out the People's Park in Halifax. It was an averagely uninteresting patch of land across the road from the Crossley mansion. They brought in earth and boulders to make a ridge of artificial hills around the perimeter and planted trees on them so that the nearby industrial buildings were shielded but the distant hills were visible over the top. A long terrace along the top was lined with statues of Roman deities and Crossley himself was commemorated by a solemn statue of himself in a pavilion that proclaims, 'Blest be the Lord who daily loadeth us with benefits.'

The most famous of these improvers was Sir Titus Salt, the founder and builder of Saltaire, to the north of Bradford. The work took place between 1850 and 1863. Salt's intentions were clear.[2] He wanted a town that would be self-sufficient. He built the factory first, the houses (792 of them) second; he never got around to building the mansion he intended for himself. It was all in the Italian Renaissance style. He built forty-five almshouses, an Institute, a school and a church and laid out a 14-acre park on the far side of the River Aire.

[1] Walter Creese, *The Search for Environment*, Yale 1966, pp. 40–6.
[2] Ibid., pp. 30–40.

The house itself had a living-room, a scullery and two to four bedrooms above them. He had no back-to-back houses, but planned rear service lanes and back-yards to each house which would contain a privy, an ashpit and a coalstore. He disliked clutter in the streets and he disliked clothes-lines even more. So clothes had to be dried in backyards; it was one answer to the problem of clothes-drying which occurs in all areas of back-to-back housing, where the washing has to be hung across the road. But Salt also set up a steam laundry, which operated at very low prices and was working until fairly recently.

He was a Congregationalist but he encouraged other churches as well. He was a philanthropist; he donated money widely; he provided funds for educa-tion; he set up schools and an institute; he employed a health officer and built an infirmary. He was opposed to alcohol, believing that it caused drunkenness, lust, crime and misery. He was the personification of Victorian paternalism.

Industrialists elsewhere followed his example. Lord Leverhulme built Port Sunlight near Liverpool from 1888. George Cadbury began building Bourn-ville in 1879; it had a slow start but grew rapidly from 1895. The original twenty-four houses became a small town, open, landscaped, thick with planting, low in density, with good gardens and houses picturesque and traditional in character. He set up an organisation for lighting, fencing and paving. But at Bournville he dropped the idea of home-ownership in favour of rentals; he discovered that the rapid appreciation in the value of the property encouraged occupiers to sell their houses and move away from the district and the factory. And that, of course, destroyed half the reason for building the place at all.

The environment created by the paternal industrialists was simple, organised and coherent. It was dominated by the factory, at first architecturally, later socially. The houses were grouped and varied to create usable common spaces and faintly decorated with styles to create a sense of belonging and identity. Nothing was elaborated for its own sake; economy and common sense underlay every aesthetic decision. Essentially—and here lay its historical significance—the project was conceived as a whole: a community of people with their houses, gardens, yards, roads, facilities, parks, recreation, schools and libraries. That cost the owners money. In Halifax, both Akroyd and Crossley received a financial return only half what the average landlord expected to make. They had, in a sense, started a social movement that must eventually lead to their own effacement.

The individual owners who made these experiments were demonstrating in a practical way an alarm that was more generally felt. In the field of public administration a similar work was in hand, less creative and positive, more regulatory and protective. Reform of housing and the environment began with controls to ensure public health.

The Sanitary Commission of 1869 to 1871 led to legislation. Local Government Boards were set up in 1871 and in 1875 was passed Disraeli's Public Health Act. It was a turning point, a major innovation in government which divided the country into rural and urban sanitary districts with defined duties. In the same year was passed the Artisans' and Labourers' Dwellings Improvement Act. The Royal Commission on the Housing of the Working Classes reported in 1884 and 1885. These and other Acts established the need for and created regulations for housing, and civic administration. In the context of this chapter the most important were the bye-laws.

Most bye-laws were passed after the Act of 1875, although in many towns and cities it was nearly the end of the century before they came into effect. They established improved criteria for the design and layout of housing and as such were beneficial. Unfortunately they also led to the building of acres of 'bye-law housing', of the type now often classified as unfit for human habitation.

Bye-law housing effectively dates from the second half of the nineteenth century. What happened was this. Under most of the bye-laws a minimum width of roads was established; for example, the front road had to be at least 24 feet wide, the back lanes at least 15 feet. The bye-laws also laid down the cubic contents of the rooms. All of these dimensions were minima. Inevitably people building to the bye-laws used the minimum width and the minimum cubic contents as if they were maxima. In the case of the rooms, since building costs tended to be lower if the room could be nearly a cube, many of the ceilings were too high and the floor areas too small. The standards were drastically revised after the Tudor Walter Report of 1918.

In terms of more co-ordinated housing layout and planning, the most important first piece of legislation was the Housing and Town Planning Act of 1909, aimed in the words of a Member of Parliament 'to secure the home healthy, the house beautiful, the town pleasant, the suburb salubrious'. The legislation was speeded up after the Great War. The Housing and Town

Planning Act of 1919 established subsidies for housing and led to the development of council housing. In 1932 was passed the Town and Country Planning Act, in which planning powers were widely extended and traffic planning was included for the first time.

Public control and private experiment thus came increasingly together. The movement might be summarised as follows. It started with protests and theories, became an ideal, led to legislation and the suppression and correction of obvious faults, and ultimately became an ideal again.

To follow that ideal we must turn to the major figure in the design of new settlements at the turn of the century. That was Raymond Unwin. He was born in 1863 and died in 1940. As a boy he had heard Ruskin lecture and had known William Morris. He pursued a consistent and logical ideal. When in 1937 he received the Gold Medal of the Royal Institute of British Architects he referred in his speech to following throughout his life 'after the ideals of a more ordered form of society and a better planned environment for it . . .'[1] For him practical planning, on a human scale, was generated only by the satisfaction of the needs of people. It was probably no accident that when the Addison axe fell on public housing after 1919 he turned his attention to building technology instead of to planning and became a founder member of the Building Research Station and ultimately its Chairman. Like Pugin, Morris and Ruskin he saw that social life and the quality of the environment were indivisible. He was a practical planner, not an academic theorist; but he recognised from the start the fundamental importance of the idea of the community and the practice of corporate life in moulding the form of the environment.

Unwin was a Christian; he emphasised the importance of Christian compassion. He was a Socialist and he believed in equality. He also believed in the natural life (whatever that may be) and sought constantly for the attainment of a social life and an environment that would be 'in close touch with realities'. He was known for his sympathy for anyone in trouble and for the indignation he would express at examples of social injustice. He was throughout influenced by the thought and writings of William Morris. Morris writing about the workman uses words that could later have come from Unwin, 'It is the province of art to set the true ideal of a full and reasonable life before him, a life to which the perception and creation of beauty, the enjoyment of real pleasure that is,

[1] Walter Creese, *The Search for Environment*, Yale 1966, pp. 158–9.

shall be felt to be as necessary to man as his daily bread . . .'[1]

What Morris defined and attempted to realise in a small way through the arts and crafts, Unwin was able to attempt on a bigger, social scale—in the field of town planning. In partnership with Barry Parker he was involved from 1900 with a programme of garden city planning and with the design of their layouts and houses.

Creese has analysed the basic principles that inspired these settlements.[2] They can be listed as follows.

1. *The village as an animate symbol*
Because of its scale and character, the village was the symbol of the natural life to which Unwin was devoted. It was a symbol both socially and aesthetically. The materials of which it was built expressed that human scale; people living in it and participating in it would thus acquire a heightened sense of peace. The village was the yardstick for community planning.

2. *The need to understand the past*
For Unwin, tradition created a language of its own; it was also a catalyst. In emphasising the importance of tradition he was following some of the main contemporary theorists of town planning. His friend Patrick Geddes, for example, insisted on the importance of the past; a plan could only be devised on the basis of a regional survey and analysis.

3. *The Middle Ages as the historic standard*
Unwin and Parker looked back to the days of the feudal lord; they had, like many artists of the time, a nostalgia for the mediaeval craftsman. Modern society, the society that had produced the grotesque industrial cities, was by nature bad; in looking for a better society, revealed by its artefacts, where else could one find it but in the Middle Ages?

4. *The indispensability of beauty*
Mental health and the existence of beauty were connected. Unwin, following his ideals further than those discussed later, was concerned not only with physical health—that would be improved by well-organised layouts, which would also be beautiful layouts; he was also concerned with mental health.

---

[1] William Morris, *How I became a Socialist*, quoted in Williams, op. cit., p. 155.
[2] Creese, op. cit., pp. 169–73.

Beauty is not something separate from life; on the contrary, a sense of locality can stimulate the development of common interests. One of his most pungent criticisms of society is his protest about the building of slums for the workers and the foundation of the Art Gallery for the people of culture. To him such specialisation of places is degrading. Art and town planning flourish together and one of the chief functions of town planning is to satisfy 'the natural aesthetic hunger of mankind'; to compartment affairs so that living is done in the slum and culture occurs in the Art Gallery is to attack the very concept of the town.

5. *Twelve houses to the acre*

This was Unwin's specific professional innovation, the technical means that co-ordinated his attitude to land and his attitude to planning. In a small book, *Nothing Gained by Overcrowding*,[1] he outlined the theory. Although he wanted cheap land and emphasised the importance of getting more for the money per family unit, any density of more than twelve houses to the acre was unnecessary. High-density planning was only relevant where the land was excessively costly. Where the prices of land were more normal, to build more than twelve houses per acre was even a financial error; the extra cost of the roads outweighed any saving in the cost of the land. In any case, twelve houses to the acre was socially a desirable density.

It accorded with his idea of the cottage as a symbol of healthy family life. If the planner wanted the planned to be in close touch with nature, and if the family was the basic unit of society, then a healthy family life must be the first priority at which the planner was aiming. A cottage, the most traditional English type of building, was both a symbol and a practical help. But many other things were essential too. The visual results of his theories included features so familiar now that they often pass unnoticed. They included the side path (the path by the side of the road or the path separated a little from it), the tree lined verge, the vista that opens and closes as the pedestrian moves through the town or the garden city, the varied set-backs of the houses, some a little way from the road, the development of focal points. By freeing the land pattern (in marked contrast with the model settlements that had preceded his) he could use the ground as an entity in itself. If, after all, the ground was important, it must be

---

[1] *Nothing Gained by Overcrowding*, published by Garden Cities and Town Planning Association, 1912, summarised in Creese, op. cit., p. 174.

accepted as a valuable element in design. Urban composition became an art in its own right. It meant an end to the tyranny of the street over the house, and the tyranny of the house over the street. For to him a town could be composed in much the same way as a picture.

He therefore engaged in a special kind of visual planning. It consisted of adjusting the solids and voids, the planes and directions, the edges, the textures and the materials so that the composition of the town was a composition of solids in space with flat foregrounds and a differentiation of plan and elevation. This involved him in changing standard regulations. He promoted a special Act of Parliament for Hampstead so that he could eliminate the bye-law street in favour of the short cul-de-sac. It was a necessary part of the total concept. All the elements put together were elements in an over-all planning sequence—from the individual, the family and the house, to the group, the community, the region and the country.

The first commission undertaken by Unwin and Parker was the planning and building of New Earswick from 1901. It was a Garden Village. The site was three miles north of York; it belonged to Rowntrees Cocoa Works.[1] They started in 1902 with twenty-eight houses designed in an appropriate English cottage style. Because of the danger of speculation and a turnover of property the houses were not sold. They were managed by a Trust. By a Trust Deed of 1904 all the profits over $3\frac{1}{2}$ per cent were returned to the Trust for the maintenance and extension of the village.

In its extended form, widely spaced, thickly planted and freely grouped around a huge central green and a Folk Hall and School, New Earswick remains today, under continuous management by the Village Trust, as near a model as a model village can be. It is difficult to appreciate how novel at the time were some of the features that now look safe and traditional. The cul-de-sac and the group of two-storey houses collected around it and its turning end are used widely. Useless pieces of back land behind the houses are eliminated by careful layout of plots and gardens. The width of roads was reduced, in turn reducing the development costs. Unwin was much concerned with the safety of children. Roads were planned to leave space for children's play. They were also, as was suitable for a garden village, named after trees.

[1] Joseph Rowntree Village Trust, *One Man's Vision*, the story of the Joseph Rowntree Village Trust, London 1954.

Houses with their ends turned to complete a view were invented here. So were many of house types. Houses with 'through' living-rooms were at the time an innovation. They made it possible to orientate the houses in many more ways than had been possible previously. Other innovations included the bathroom on the first floor, the elimination of winders from the stairs, the outside store built into the house (for fuel, prams, tools and almost anything else) and the flanking walls which were later incorporated to create a visual unity for the village as a whole, not just for the house and its garden.

He had developed a basic layout and went on trying to improve on it. Moving into York itself between 1926 and 1936 he built the Clifton Lodge Estate. Working class patterns worked out at New Earswick were transformed into middle class patterns. The houses cost between £1,500 and £1,650, but now there were only 4½ houses to the acre. The gardens were larger and lusher,

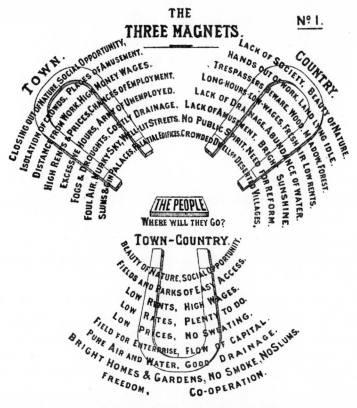

Ebenezer Howard: the Three Magnets

the houses still essentially cottages. He introduced the through sitting-room with three exposures, with 'the object of securing an unusual amount of sunnyness, cheerfulness, brightness and openness'. In applying such concepts to the design of mass repetitive housing, he set a standard. The cottages, quiet and unassuming, were a logical deduction from a social ideal.

If Unwin was the practitioner, Ebenezer Howard was the theorist. He was neither an architect nor a planner. In 1898 he published *Tomorrow: a Peaceful Path to Real Reform*, reissued a few years later under the title *Garden Cities of Tomorrow*.[1] Howard is the principal exponent of the theory of the garden city which Unwin worked out in practice. In one of his most memorable diagrams he contrasts the three magnets—town, country, and (his own magnet) town country. He aimed at 'slumless, smokeless cities', and introduced the idea of the garden city, which would have the advantages of both town and country and the disadvantages of neither. It was to be 'a town designed for healthy living and industry; of a size that makes possible a full measure of social life, but not larger; surrounded by a permanent belt of rural land; the whole of the land being held in public ownership or held in trust for the community'.

Fundamentally, therefore, Howard's proposal was complementary to Unwin's. If Unwin's was a vision of the form and function of the garden city, Howard's was of an exercise in co-operative ownership. The two ideas were linked, particularly as regards the maintenance of the environment and its long-term value as an investment.

Letchworth, started in 1903 and the first example of the developed garden city, proved the point.[2] Those who invested money obtained interest on their capital of 4 to 5 per cent; the remainder of the income was used for local improvements and for the benefit of the community. Howard had laid out the financial structure for development. Seven years after the incorporation of a joint stock company a body of trustees could purchase the stock at par; the town could thus be run by its own community. He did not entirely foresee what would happen. The town was successful and attracted prosperity. The freeholds increased rapidly in value, but the limitation on the dividends prevented the distribution of gains. In the long term, therefore, Letchworth became highly attractive for a takeover bid; by 1962 it was necessary to pass the

[1] Ebenezer Howard, *Garden Cities of Tomorrow*, 1902, new edition London 1946.
[2] Creese, op. cit., Chapter 9, pp. 203–18.

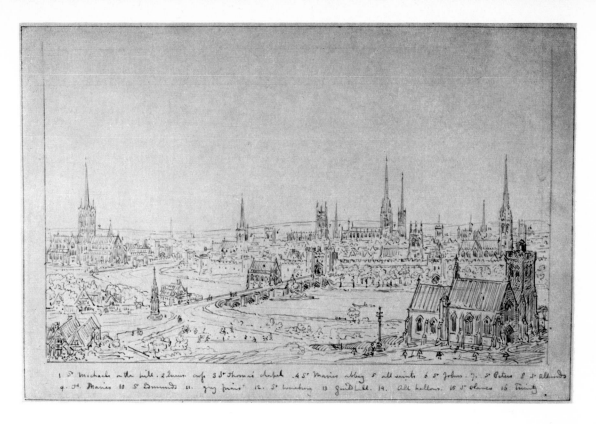

1 S¹ Michaels on the hill. 2 hmm asp 3 S¹ Thomas chapel. 4 S¹ Maries abbey 5 all saints 6 S¹ Johns. 7. S¹ Peters 8 S¹ Albunds
9 S¹ Maries 10 S¹ Edmunds 11. gray friars 12. S¹ lowrkey 13 guidhall. 14. All hallow. 15 S¹ Olaves 16 Trinity

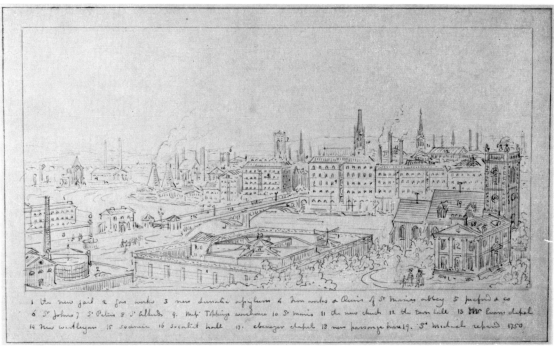

1 the new jail 2 gas works 3 new lunatic asylum 4 iron works & ruins of S¹ Maries abbey 5 pucford & co
6 S¹ Johns 7 S¹ Peters 8 S¹ Albunds 9 M¹ T Akkings warehouse 10 S¹ maries 11 the new church 12 the town hall 13 M¹ Evans chapel
14 new wesleyan 15 socenian 16 socialist hall 17. ebenezer chapel 18 new parsonage house 19. S¹ Michaels repaired 1750.

34. From Pugin's *Contrasts*: a town of 1440 contrasted with the same town in 1840.
(From the original drawings) (p. 83)

35.
Boston Spa,
Yorkshire (p. 80)

Keith Gibson

Keith Gibs

36. Copley, near Halifax (p. 87)

37.
Halifax: the People's
Park (p. 88)

Keith Gibson

Keith Gibson

38. Halifax: Akroydon (Boothtown) (pp. 87–88)

39. Saltaire, Shipley, Yorkshire (pp. 88–89)

Keith Gibson

40. Leeds: a 19th-century back street (p. 90)

Keith Gibson

41. York: on the Clifton Lodge Estate (p. 95)

Keith Gibson

42. New Earswick, near York: the garden village (pp. 94–95)

43. Cumbernauld New Town (p. 97)

44.
California: a clover-
leaf crossing
(pp. 100–101)

Aerofilms

45. Leeds: continuous modern development (p. 103)

Letchworth Garden City Corporation Act, which made Letchworth a statutory corporation managed for the benefit of the community. Howard had established, long after his death, that good planning makes for increased values; that it also brought in the people who wish to make a quick profit by speculating in it was a tribute to the financial soundness of his theory. A good and humane environment catering for people's needs is not the enemy of a sound economy in the long term.

With that incident this interpretation of the common or garden city is complete. But it is worth adding that, as Creese has shown, it is to this movement that the British New Towns built after the 1939–45 War belong. In many ways they reviewed the themes that had been developed by Parker and Unwin. They were concerned with making a visual picture, with building upon tradition, with recapturing the spirit of the village; they belonged to the family of the garden cities, to the acceptance of the identity of social and aesthetic improvement. They were based upon an idea—the 'balanced community'—and were essentially attempts at community planning.

Lord Reith was chairman of the Commission on the New Towns that reported in 1946; in that year also the New Towns Act was passed. Reith was able, in a feat surely unique in the history of planning, to extract from the members of his commission a unanimous view on the principles to be followed in planning a new town.

The towns were to have a population of between 50,000 and 100,000. They were to be low in density, surrounded by a green belt and separated from big existing cities. They were to be threaded through with green spaces. There was to be a mixture of housing types, though mainly they would have two-storey terraced housing. The most important principle however was the neighbourhood principle. This was an attempt to break down the overall size of the town into units of the right size for a community. 10,000 people appeared to be a reasonable size, but it also worked well because 10,000 people provided the right number of children for a secondary modern school, for two two-stream primary schools and for six nursery schools. Five neighbourhoods of 10,000 each gave 50,000 people and that would be enough people to provide the right number of children for a grammar school. The school system therefore became one of the determinants of social planning. Physically the plan could be based upon distances appropriate for the school; children going to nursery school might be expected to walk a quarter of a mile and spend about five minutes in doing so, children going to a primary school might have to walk half a mile and spend ten minutes, children going to a secondary school might go considerably further. At its centre the neighbourhood had a centre with shops, perhaps a community centre and a public house. The over-all size of the neighbourhood was dictated by the maximum walking distance for a woman with a pram from the community centre or the neighbourhood centre to her house.

The components of the new community were thus the dwelling house and its density, the school and its distance, the social centre and its centrality. The ideal, after all, was of 'a balanced community enjoying a full social, industrial and commercial life'. Through a coherent movement the planning of the environment had come of age.

In 1909 the Housing and Town Planning Act defined its purpose as 'to secure proper sanitary conditions, amenity and convenience'. Postwar planning might be summarised as 'the study and control of factors physical, social, economic and aesthetic with a view to their integration and improvement for the benefit of the community'.

6 The Man in the Clover Leaf

The title of this chapter comes from the book by Harvey Cox, *The Secular City*.[1] The sub-title of the book is *Secularisation and Urbanisation in Theological Perspective*; it is the work of a theologian and it is very relevant to the problems of urban planning today. As such it is a significant contribution to the growing literature about urbanisation which started with Weber in 1899.

The starting point for the argument of this chapter is the growth of cities.[2] On a world scale the speed of population growth is now twice what it was in 1940: the world population has doubled since 1900 and it is likely to double again in thirty-five years. By the year 2,100 we can expect the world to have between six and seven thousand million people. The implications of this are considerable. The total value of the building stock created in the next forty years should equal the total created in the last 6,000 years. Where however will most people be? By the end of this century 2,600 million people will live in settlements that have a population of more than one million; at present only 370 million do so. They will be mainly new settlements; for the cities in the under-developed countries expanded in the decade from 1950 to 1960 a third faster than the cities in the developed countries. At their present rate of expansion they will double in size and population every fifteen years. It is possible to forecast cities of fifty to sixty million people in India by the end of this century, the equivalent of the entire population of Great Britain in one city.

This is the emerging world of the new urban man, very small in an

[1] Harvey Cox, *The Secular City*, SCM Press, London 1965.
[2] See Kingsley Davis, *The Urbanisation of the Human Population*, in *Cities*: A 'Scientific American' Book, London 1965, pp. 11–32.

extravagantly huge environment. In that sense he is like the man at Delphi facing nature across the valley. But now he is a man without the beliefs and the ideologies that would make for him a natural place in the environment and a natural relationship to the external world. For the external world is increasingly man-made.

Cox gives two images to describe the characteristics of this urban man—his anonymity and his mobility. First, he is the man at the giant switchboard; he is anonymous, enmeshed in a network of communications. Secondly, he is the man in the clover leaf; he is mobile, moving in a system.[1]

The clover leaf is the complicated large scale traffic intersection using curving lanes and several levels which enables a driver to take a new direction without crossing a single line of traffic. It is as yet more common in America than in Britain and is therefore a more immediate image. It is in many ways an image of a city because the modern metropolis is itself a system of roads and other forms of communication linking and unlinking horizontally and vertically.

But it is possible to take the image further than Cox does. For what happens at a clover leaf crossing? The crossing is complex and based on calculations of flow. It is man-made, constructed of reinforced concrete, and highly artificial. The driver changes direction without interruption from other vehicles and his speed is approximately constant. The only technical problem is estimating a weaving distance for moving into and out of a moving stream of traffic. The idea is to move into another stream without forcing someone else to stop his own career; he merely comes into vision and disappears again into obscurity.

Whatever the vehicle, technology is in control of the situation. If there is a mechanical failure, society comes to a halt as all the vehicles pile up. But what about the individual man? The man himself is enclosed and isolated in his little tin box. Each man exists only for himself, each is moving in his own chosen direction. Communication can only be established by signs—signs that have been classified, categorised and approved by society. Urban man thus moves in a world dictated by construction and by management.

We can take the image still further. Where is the man in the car going? He must know in advance. He is wholly dependent upon the instructions in the vehicle and on the road, and he has to be able to read information rapidly. If he fails to look out of the window to read the instructions correctly or takes a

[1] Cox, op. cit., pp. 51–4.

wrong turning he may have to travel many miles before he can get back into the right stream. He is dominated by movement and speed. It is also a world in which individualism does not pay; however isolated he may be in his container he must conform to the rules; there can be no place for the nonconformist in the modern traffic system.

As a physical situation it is unprecedented in history. Equally unprecedented is the scale of the operation. Take the area of land additional to the motorway which is necessary for such a crossing. A grade-separated roundabout occupies between 6 and 10 acres. A full clover leaf crossing requires 60 to 80 acres. The size increases with the complexity. In the 1960s a four-level intersection was built in Los Angeles which occupied 80 acres, that is, the area of the centre of an English New Town. Even more vivid is a comparison of the area needed for the crossing with a similar area used for housing. If housing were built even at a low density of fifteen houses per acre, the area occupied by a crossing of 60 acres would be enough for 900 houses, or homes for about 3,000 people.

Here then is a world which is man-made, dominated by technology and made possible by power. It is characterised by movement and flow, by the need for technical information and a know-how recognised by society, by conformity to the patterns that that society demands. The person dependent upon or subject to all these forces is urban or technopolitan man, herded into privacy and isolation, hopelessly dwarfed by the huge scale that technology requires. He is the man in the clover leaf and he contrasts with the man in the fig leaf, the man living in nature and simplicity with God around the corner.

The man in the clover leaf can also be seen as symptomatic of the city as a whole. For the first characteristic of the modern city is the disappearance of recognisable boundaries. Throughout history, until the twentieth century, the city had a limited catchment area for people and a recognisable zone of influence. It operated as a market and its economics could be understood fairly simply. The Industrial Revolution and the railways reinforced its centrality and its concentrated form. But with new forms of transport, particularly the private car, and the increase in mobility, the catchment area has been enormously enlarged. The residential area of the city is no longer limited fundamentally by proximity to work. The city may be recognised as the nucleus of a city region which spreads much further than the city itself, but there may be more than one city and certainly more than one town or village in such a region. The container no longer contains. The city as such is no longer a social reality.

That is in keeping with what has been happening to the components of the city too. If Unwin could see a sequence of recognisable units from the house to the country, expanding like rings in a pool from the splash of a stone, such a convenient categorisation is no longer possible. Perhaps because of shortage of space, individual components are more multipurpose and their limits less clear. The gadget in the kitchen does more than one operation, the rooms in the house can change their functions, the house is not separate from the garden, the gardens are often fused together in open space, the open space infiltrates the town and the town and countryside are no longer distinct as each takes on some of the characteristics of the other. It is a small intellectual step from here to regions and nations and international linkages.

It follows that many of the traditional concepts are obsolete, and the verbal categories into which places could conveniently be put—country, village, town, city—and which provided the security of knowing where one was, have been eroded away. And any local independence left by the improvement of physical communications has been eroded still further by electronic communications.

In such an urban world, of widespread functions, of mass communications, of networks of activities rather than centres of living, the second major characteristic of the modern city is its subjection to continuous functional change. And that has an immediate effect upon the roles of the people involved in it.

In the book referred to above, Harvey Cox uses a distinction drawn by Cornelis Van Peursen, the sociologist who holds the chair of philosophy at the University of Leiden. Van Peursen is concerned with the relationship between types of society and ways of perceiving reality. He divides history into three eras; the mythical, the ontological and the functional (described by Cox as tribal, town and technopolitan respectively). In the mythical era people are fascinated by reality, and explanations are given in mythological terms. In the ontological era the fear of magic is replaced by an understanding of the sacred as separated from the profane; things are seen as essences, and the polis and the town emerged.

In the functional area, emerging now, 'only that which is directly related to us is real. Things do not exist in themselves; they are no longer substances, but they exist in and for the sake of what they do with us and what we do with them.' Things become things to do; we are interested in thinking rather than in thought, in acting justly rather than in the abstract nature of justice, in the act of loving rather than in love itself. To quote Van Peursen again, 'in the period of myth, the main issue was *that* something is; in the period of ontological thinking, it was *what* something is; in the period of functional thinking, it is *how* something is, how it functions'.[1]

Of few areas of life is this more true than in that of urban development. What dictates the changing form of the city and the location and type of its houses is less and less a vision of its totality, more and more an assembly of requirements and necessities. As the population increases and the pressures upon space become greater the conditions in which building or planning can take place become more dominant. There are limitations of the site, dictating whether one can build high or low, limitations of cost, crucial to the form of buildings, limitations of intent, established by the client's needs and wants, and limitations by regulation—street widths, fire regulations, bye-laws and insurance. It is, in McLuhan's familiar phrase, an environment in which the medium is the message.

Who, then, controls the constant change? It is a situation in which only the professional can know what is happening or what is the reason why a place takes on the form it has. It is a world in which expert knowledge in a technical field is essential: a world of experts and of specialists. It becomes more difficult year by year for experts from different specialisms to understand each other; a lay committee making decisions about towns is even more helpless in the face of expert opinion about traffic, about planning, about commercial forecasting and analysis.

But the professional planner is somehow required to be an expert in making a synthesis of all of them. To do that he must have an all-embracing, clear objective, large enough to bring together in a unit all the components of urban living. There seems to me only one possible objective. It is essentially to ensure a place with dignity for the individual as the core and determinant of the new environment. It involves a reversal of any situation in which the individual is not the master of the environment but its victim, in danger of being submerged in a sub-human landscape, dwarfed by mass, directed by power and poisoned by pollution.

That requires conscious planning. There is no evidence in history that an environment satisfying to man and fulfilling his individual and social needs

[1] Ibid., pp. 64–5.

ever emerges from an uncontrolled exploitation of the land for immediate gain. Every positive and satisfactory environment (such as those discussed in previous chapters) has involved an idea and taken shape under control of some kind. The idea towards which this chapter is moving is that of an environment centred upon man—a new landscape of humanism, but a humanism of all men, not only of those with authority and wealth.

To turn from analysis to prescription, what does this idea imply? It implies that any humane environment must find its origin in a consideration of the needs of the man and not in that of the clover leaf. But the needs of the man are not just personal and insular. He is involved at all levels and at all periods in his life in relationships with other people. The starting point for a concept of the environment is thus, not a man alone (or even a man in a motor car) but the individual in society.

Civilisation depends, after all, upon human contact and speech. Dialogue between individuals is necessary, and especially necessary in a democracy. Democracy cannot exist or survive without that dialogue; and yet the modern city, despite its astonishing communications, can easily make people more isolated. It is the quality of the relationships between people that characterise the society. A humane concept of the city must therefore emphasise man in society, not man subject to technology: the individual and the family, not the amorphous crowd: human scale, not that of the machine.

The basis for the planning of the modern city has, it follows, to be an understanding of man himself. And that involves, not a partial familiarity with a few measurable factors, but an understanding derived both from individual experience and from a synthesis of the ever-growing studies in the social and environmental sciences. It involves the study of man in his habitat, as the centre of an ecological system—the principal part of a science that examines the habits of living organisms in relation to their surroundings.

The planner and theorist who has in this century made the most practical contribution to the working out of this idea is Constantinos Doxiadis, head of Doxiadis Associates and of the Athens Centre of Ekistics. Ekistics is the science of human settlements. In a number of books, such as *Architecture in Transition, The New World of Urban Man, Urban Renewal and the Future of the American City,* and the comprehensive and monumental *Ekistics,*[1] Doxiadis has made an

[1] C. A. Doxiadis, *Architecture in Transition*, London 1963; *The New World of Urban*

analysis of existing settlements and attempted a synthesis of the elements in the new city, a concept of the emerging world-scale settlement, ecumenopolis. Whilst in no way reflecting the scope and quality of his studies, the remainder of this chapter is mainly derived from them and from thoughts provoked by them.

If the individual in society is the determinant of the plan, it follows that it must be built up from him as the basic unit. Start with the individual alone. How big should his unit be? Edward T. Hall describes the minimum human space for a living being as his 'bubble'.[1] That is an invisible space whose boundaries can be drawn round a man's extremities; it constantly changes its shape with his actions, as he reaches out for things or withdraws; and it is affected by the situation he finds himself in. The bubble of a man alone with his arms held out will be wide and round; the bubbles of a lot of people huddled together in a crowd are squeezed together narrowly but may project upwards if all they can do is raise their hands.

The bubble is a man's 'personal' distance. But distances which are 'social' can also be measured. They would be very close at four to seven feet; more acceptable at seven to twelve feet. The dimensions necessary for two people are more significant for planning than those necessary for one person. For example, the ideal distance for conversation between two people sitting in chairs is one in which they could just touch if they reached out to do so; that is, they could pass things.

On that basis we might work out the most desirable dimensions for a room. But a room is rarely used for one purpose only; as the uses become more varied and complex and the numbers of people larger, a range of dimensions can be assembled. They will be modified, and other requirements noted, by a consideration of other factors—for example, acoustics, heat and ventilation, light, and (the most elusive as well as the most important) the increasingly known preferences of different social groups.

The next stage is the house and its immediate surroundings. Immediately, the number of factors involved increases dramatically. Distance, for example,

---

Man, Boston 1965; *Urban Renewal and the Future of the American City*, Chicago 1966; *Ekistics*, London 1968.

[1] Edward T. Hall, *The Hidden Dimension*, New York 1966.

is no longer a relatively simple item. The distance between a mother looking out from an upper floor in a multi-storey block and her child playing on the ground, is not the literal distance but the psychological distance, which includes the time it takes to go down the stairs if the child is in danger, or to wait for the lift.

Similar factors may affect the layout of an area. The maximum size for a town square, suggests Doxiadis, is one which makes it possible to recognise someone on the other side of the square. That is a distance of about 100 yards. It is the size of one of the ancient stadia in Greece or Rome and of many of the most satisfactory market places. To bring the scale still nearer to the individual, it may be important to recognise, not only a face, but a facial expression; the maximum distance for that is said to be 70 feet. On a smaller scale yet, the desirable width for a pavement may be one which will make it possible for two couples to pass each other without inconvenience; that will require 12 feet.

Again, there are factors such as noise. It should be possible for two people to hold a conversation on a pavement without the noise of traffic making it intolerable; that may affect the location of pedestrian ways. To reduce the noise passing across a courtyard may suggest surfacing the court with grass rather than sound-reflective paving; that affects the choice of materials. Again, there is increasing information on the microclimate, on the effects of air currents created by the shape and location of buildings; that may lead to a regrouping of elements and to more controlled environments—enclosed, warm shopping precincts with calculated movements of air and levels of noise.

At this scale, as more is known about the different factors, the more are they seen to affect one another, and the more multi-purpose are many of the traditional details of the urban scene. They become important for measurable reasons, not only because they are part of history. The trees and hedges in the streets are not just attractive to look at; they are necessary climatically. The small patches of open space, the soft areas, the grass, as well as the more obvious parks and green belts, are essential to the maintenance of sound levels, the absorption of pollutants, the movement of fresh air, as well as to the promotion of social activities. Pedestrian streets, alleys and the breaks in them, the seats and furniture, the rails, posts, brackets, lampposts and litterbins, are not only fun to look at and immediately useful; they also provide recognisable features, on a human scale, that can be touched as well as seen and incorporated in a person's perception of a particular place. Play areas for children not only answer many of these needs; they also bring together all age groups and provide them with something in common.

If the study of human needs can lead to a number of desiderata for the layout of an area, it can also provide desiderata for a whole settlement. But now other factors come into play; on this scale time may be more significant than distance. Take the problem of travel to and from work. The ordinary day of 24 hours is divided into three equal periods of 8 hours each—8 hours working, 8 hours sleeping, and 8 hours leisure. Despite all the changes in society, there appears to be little that can be done about the two first; the tendencies in the modern city lead to the erosion of the third. Travel consumes an increasing proportion of it, and in some cases nearly all of it as commuters travel through several settlements before coming to the one they want. But this is more than an inconvenience. The eight hours for leisure includes the time available for social activity and creative work; its erosion must affect the quality of society. A plan must therefore make some assumptions about what is a maximum reasonable travelling distance or—more important—travelling time.

These factors are selected as examples, almost at random, of the processes of study that may lead to the assembling of a systematic list of human needs in the urban environment. Is it likely that such a study will suggest any answers to the questions raised by the design of cities? In Doxiadis' view, it is possible to meet the human requirements by the design of a cell for urban living; and this he defines as an 'ekistic unit'.

One of the larger ekistic units is the physical expression of a community. For in a square 2,000 metres long in each direction it is possible to accommodate 50,000 people. Nearly all will be within ten minutes of the centre; and ten minutes is an acceptable average walking time for most people. By adding such cells together, a system is developed. A car, also taking ten minutes, can give access to many cells. For many people ten minutes may be enough; but those prepared to drive for two hours (which many people do now) could reach all parts of a very big settlement. But even within the limit of ten minutes, different forms of transport make many ranges of contact possible. There is a man on foot, on a bicycle, in a car, finally in an aeroplane.

It is not difficult to see that such an approach to the planning of a settlement has a profound effect upon one's idea of what a settlement is. It is one moreover peculiar to our age. The idea of cells is central to modern scientific discovery, and it applies to other areas of life—to space and its capsules, to structures, to all kinds of networks. The linking of one cell to another creates the network. In the case of the urban settlement, the totality has then no meaning, no centre and no edges. It is open-ended and continuous, and ultimately synonymous with the world. As that happens, the cell takes on its full significance as the unit for a man's immediate experience and for a community of men, within the limits of human measurement. The conclusion is the same as that for many other areas in human affairs—that what is significant today is not the size of the whole but the size of the units of which it is composed. In the midst of a dynamic, constantly growing and changing collection of linked settlements, the units can be relatively static and always recognisable.

Such an idea of the modern urban environment seems to me rich with promise, giving scope not just for development but for the continuity of history and the retention of the old as a constituent part of the new. Old, well worn and humane towns, which have not exploded beyond the size that they can sustain without confusion, become units or cells within the unending city. The cities which have the most questionable future are those which have already distorted their past—the monster cities that now need to be fragmented and cut through with open spaces and new communication lines and whose elements need to be rediscovered. It was the attempt to make an old small city cope with all the demands of the modern technological world that caused their confusion. The attempt was a logical absurdity; a city centre rebuilt to accommodate all the motor cars that come to it would have no space left for the city centre itself. The process of indefinite radial growth is self-destructive.

As part of a network, with links and spaces, the human-scale settlement has a more positive future. The old is not just a piece of history or even just part of a continuum; it is a necessary component. And that means that it is essential to the idea of the environment. To benefit from it means seeing the environment as one composed of the past as well as the present and the future. Planning involves, with each generation, a new experience of place and form. Each generation needs to rediscover its environment and redesign it with the past as an essential part of the new total concept—a new idea of an urban space in which the old buildings are a living part of the whole, an environment reflecting all phases of history and meeting the needs of all ages of people.

In the places where most things are new, increasing knowledge and a more profound science require us, not to make more repellent environments, but to recognise in their design the essential needs of continuity, of conservation, of adopting a more ecological approach to the total environment—one that sees it as part of a system of change, of growth and decay. The sub-human modern environment is the partial solution, dictated by expediency, inevitably short-lived. The new environment requires a more profound link with reality; and that, if these chapters are valid, implies the manipulation of nature through design, discovering its richness and bending its potentialities to the realisation of a new order and beauty.

Index

Index